More Praise for Out oi

"More than a story of survival, this book is a story of a beautiful metamorphosis. I enjoyed this journey immensely, as anyone would who cheers for the underdog and applauds those who cross the finish line in glory. May we all emerge out of the madness! This book is illuminating."

Brian Luke Seaward, Author of *Stand Like Mountain, Flow Like Water: Reflections on Stress and Human Spirituality*

"In *Out of the Madness: A Message of Hope*, Saf Buxy shares his lifelong struggle through addiction to wholeness. He reveals his wrenching life lessons and the insights he learned so that we too can arise through our own challenges. Saf's incredible true story is engaging and absorbing. The details are vivid, the people and places are tangible. It's like we're there. This well-crafted book also vividly renditions Saf's experiences of racism, making his book even more momentous. Through his suffering, he rose into his higher purpose so we also might find strength through our ordeals and emerge as heroes of our own journeys. Saf Buxy's journey from London's East End in the 1970s to serving humanity is truly inspiring."

Charol Messenger, author of *Your Awakening Attitude of Service,* and honoree of Marquis Who's Who in America 2020

"If you look at living your life in a world of possibility like I do, you will enjoy Saf Buxy's book *Out of the Madness: A Message of Hope.* His life's story is filled with remarkable resilience and hope. I am inspired with his remarkable creativity!"

Elsie Ritzenhein, Bestselling author of *Awakening Your Creative Voice - Women in a World of Possibility*

"Saf Buxy's book takes you on a journey through his darkest hours to his metamorphosis and rebirth. The resulting energy and resilience to give to others in sacred leadership is part of humanity's journey out of the darkness to this new era. This book can inspire you to share your gifts too!"

Sharron Rose, Producer and Director of Quantum Qi, author of *The Path of the Priestess*

"I read Saf Buxy's autobiography, *Out of the Madness: A Message of Hope*, as a remarkable journey out of his unconsciousness to a mindful, fulfilling life. I understand to get to the highest tops, one must explore the deepest depths. As a Radical Mindfulness Expert, I am impressed by his remarkable turnaround to a high contributor to help others free themselves from addiction and pain."

Daniel Gutierrez, bestselling author of *Radical Mindfulness*

"This is a book you should read and won't forget – and not because of its 'happy ending'. Saf Buxy graphically describes his 33 years of horrifying addiction and abuse (of both self and others) so compellingly that you can't believe that there could ever be a 'happy ending' to his story – or that anyone carrying this level of self-destructive trauma could eventually write about it so coherently.

But here it is, a testimony to our ultimate instinct to surrender to our creator's grace and allow its infinite power to 'miraculously' intervene in an otherwise 'unredeemable' life of self-sabotage. The resulting transformation: completely turning Saf's life of intractable 'Madness' into today's remarkable service to humanity and his devoted support to those seeking to make themselves 'whole' again, no matter how 'Mad' their circumstances.

You won't forget the book because it will shatter your deepest assumptions about life and how it all works – and you won't believe it until you do!"

Dr. William Spady, Leadership and Transformational Outcome-Based Education (TOBE), author of ***Outcome-Based Education's Empowering Essence***

"We are in the midst of a planetary transformation and opening to the beauty and wonder of a New Earth. Many illuminated people, like Saf Buxy, are having dramatic journeys of awakening during these times. His book, ***Out of the Madness: A Message of Hope,*** is a powerful example of a person who has dared to turn his life around and shine his love into the world."

Kiara Windrider, author of ***Gaia Luminous*** and ***Homo Luminous***

"It takes great courage to face the demons of our past and tell the world of its deepest, darkest sufferings. Saf Buxy takes the reader inside little known world of growing up Indian on the streets of London and how dreaming for a better life led him down a path of drugs and crime until he had a final wake-up call. Saf's story is evidence that even the harshest past can lead to new life."

Victoria Reynolds, Spiritual Luminary and author of ***Transcending Fear, Free Your Spirit and Own Your True Worth***

"If you are someone who roots for the underdog, then this book is for you. ***Out of the Madness: A Message of Hope,*** by Saf Buxy, is authentic and raw. His challenges lead him on a soul searching journey of hope. Similar to my story in ***Love@Work: The Essential Guide to a Life of Inspired Purpose***, Saf's life story concludes with him helping others by communicating his message of hope. I applaud how he has pushed through tremendous difficulties to find his inspired purpose."

Olivia Parr-Rud, author of ***Love@Work: The Essential Guide to a Life of Inspired Purpose***

Out of the Madness

Saf Buxy

Mason Works Press

Out of the Madness
A Message of Hope
by Saf Buxy

Published by Mason Works Press - Boulder, Colorado, USA.

For information, please contact Kathy Mason, Publisher, at:
kathy@masonworksmarketing.com

or write to:

Mason Works Press
6525 Gunpark Dr. #370-426
Boulder, CO 80301

Disclaimer: While the publisher and author have used their best efforts in preparing this book, they make no representations or warranties with respect to its accuracy or completeness. In addition, this book contains no legal or medical advice; please consult a licensed professional if appropriate.

For reasons that are obvious, the names used in the telling of Saf Buxy's story have either been eliminated, or in some cases only nicknames have been used. In no way does he wish to malign or slander anyone who is a part of his story, and it is for this reason that this story has been told in this way.

First Edition

ISBN: 978-0-9983209-5-3
Library of Congress Control Number: Pending

Cover Design: Eugene Stickney, Kathy Mason, and Maryann Sperry
Editorial and Interior Design Layout: Jim Rogers
Artwork on page 10: Sal Knights

Published in the United States of America

ACKNOWLEDGEMENTS

For their contributions, encouragement, and patience, I'd like to thank the following individuals who either helped or inspired me to write this book.

First of all, I'd like to thank my wife Mehz; daughter, Aaliyah; son, Zayd; and my mummy and pops, Shahida and Yusuf; along with the rest of my family, for their support as I set about writing my story.

Secondly, I'd like to thank Kathy Mason for all of her patience and assistance in helping me bring this into reality.

Thirdly, I'd like to thank Fred Atkins who has been involved with this project from the start and assisted me throughout. This would not have been possible without him.

Finally, I'd like to thank each individual I've worked with as they have all given me an even greater reason to share my story of experience, strength, and hope with the world.

A special shout out to Naeem and Farida who supported my family emotionally near the end of my madness, played a significant role in my early recovery, and continue to do so.

An immense sense of thanks to my therapist Lynn Hunt who totally gets me and for whom I'll always be grateful.

Last, but not least, I would also like to honor my close friend and humanitarian partner at "Healing for the Nations", Tania Simmons, who constantly motivates, inspires, and encourages me to be the best that I can be.

Thank you for believing in me.

I would like to dedicate this book to my loved one's who are no longer with me:

Amena Buxy (Ma)
Esmail Buxy (Daddy)
Abdulhusain Saboowalla (Uncle)
Zakir Rajulawalla (Bruv)
Asif Zojwalla
Lord Noon
Shirin Challawala
Shabbir Hatimi
Ikbal Rajulawalla
Chris Moore
Simon Withrington
Pete Brandon

FOREWORD

This is a story about abuse and how to survive it... how I survived it.

It's a story of the fallout and damage that abuse causes over time as the victim tries to cope.

It's also a story of how racial, sexual, and emotional abuse can lead to addiction... to alcohol and worse.

It's also about how you can cope when coping seems impossible.

Even more so, it's a story of coming through the other side and refusing to allow one's past to define their future.

Ultimately, it's about how you can survive, overcome, and thrive.

My name is Saf Buxy. I'm a grateful survivor, thriver, and so much more.

This is my story.

Out of the

SAF BUXY

Contents

INTRODUCTION

ADDICTION IN THE FORMS of alcoholism and illicit drug abuse is a phenomenon that continues to explode the world over.

In previous centuries, an alcoholic or addict was often relegated to a sanitarium where one would 'dry out', only to re-enter society and begin the cycle of alcoholism once again. For the alcoholic/addict, this was the hamster wheel that most found themselves on until their life finally ended.

In the late 1930s this would change with the founding, by Bill W. and Dr. Bob, of Alcoholics Anonymous, also known as AA, a spiritually based program of recovery from alcoholism. Since then, the program has since spun off into other programs of recovery from other addictions including those to narcotics, gambling, sex, and even compulsive eating and food.

With a proven road to recovery now in place, this made it possible for many who would have been hopeless addicts to turn their lives around through the help of "a power greater than themselves."

Ultimately, the above was very good news for those who had been struggling with addiction without a way out of their own life of madness.

However, individuals in recovery would relapse, falling back into their old patterns as they did. As this continued, more and more was learned about the disease that we know as addiction. In essence, what was learned is that most of those who deal with addiction happen to have other factors involved (also known as co-morbid conditions) that make ending their addiction an even greater challenge unless, and until, such conditions are addressed.

In addition to a deep, unresolved, emotional pain, which could have been the result of an emotionally disconnected childhood (in an alcoholic home), some of the other factors include low self-esteem, chronic sexual and emotional abuse, mental illness (whether bipolar disorder, schizophrenia, depression, anxiety, or PTSD), genetics, pressure and stress, an unstable home environment, social factors (such as rebelliousness and bullying), along with an appeal to the lifestyle of someone who abuses substances. Three other factors that contribute to drug addiction are:

- A lack of emotional attachment with the child by a parent or primary caregiver
- Ineffective or non-existent parenting
- Exposure to a caregiver who uses drugs or alcohol

Additionally, some substance abuse (marijuana and tobacco, for two) is also driven by the condition known as attention deficit hyperactivity disorder, or ADHD.

Many of the above conditions are what I finally realized were present in my own life, either past or present, as it spiralled out of control.

This book is a chronicle of my struggles, along with a few of the very crazy, strange, and truly bizarre experiences that were a part of my life while I was an active addict. I share these not to glorify that part of my life and the accompanying lifestyle, but to help you understand that addiction has many contributing factors, or 'causes', while it also has a way out that can lead the addict into a much happier, fulfilling, and productive life.

However, I also have come to believe that one other factor contributed to my addictions... being adopted. Please don't misunderstand me when I say this. I'm not in any way condemning adoption, as many who have been adopted have led wonderful, happy, healthy lives. Yet for some, the questions that never get answered, along with a lack of emotional attachment to one's parents in their early years, can also add to the cauldron of conditions that are responsible for addictions in someone's life. I know that it did in mine.

Above all, this book is my story into, through, and out of addiction... and into an incredibly amazing life. This healing has given me a real second chance at life with my wonderful wife and children, as well as a new career that I've built around helping others make their way through (and out of) their own madness. While I'm here to tell you that it's no easy task to begin, it's also one that is VERY rewarding and worth every ounce of your effort.

May you find in the following pages, not only entertainment, but also perhaps a few "I get that," moments. What I've learned since becoming clean and sober is that my past is my past. While I can't change that, I can embrace it to help others learn from my mistakes.

Turn the page.

School is now in session.

1

A FACEFUL OF DEODORANT

The attackers were white, thick-set, shaven-headed, and anywhere between the ages of 19 and 35, which meant that the authorities had a shortlist of around 5,000 suspects in our neighbourhood alone.

They walked into the shop, sprayed deodorant in my father's face, and robbed him while he struggled to regain his sight. As this was happening, I was cowering behind the shelves, ashamed that I wasn't doing anything to help him, even though I was *only five years old*.

Just quite what a five-year-old was supposed to do against a neanderthal in jackboots with swastika tattoos was a question I never actually asked myself at the time, but I still felt like a coward.

Whilst all that my father could do was try to defend himself, by the time he'd managed to open his eyes they'd already gone.

In actuality, the 'Met' (the English police) were significantly nicer than you'd expect. At the time they were all 6'2" and "proper geezers," who genuinely wanted to help us. The institutional racism only came later as the demographics of the area changed and the

black and Asian communities started to take the blame for the rising
levels of crime.

"Paki-bashing," as it was known at the time, was a fact of life in
England in the late 1970s… something that was especially acute in
London's East End, where the Asians were taking over from the Jews
as the target of choice for the young men (and they were *almost
always men*) who needed someone to blame for their own failing,
inadequate lives.

As an almost stereotypical Asian shopkeeper, whose life was
entirely devoted to his shop, my father was an easy target. His culture
demanded that he support his family — and to do that he worked
from daybreak till well after dark.

Forty years later I'm still wondering if the attack was entirely
racially motivated, or if the abuse they showered on my father was
just an added bonus for them.

The 'P-word' (Paki) became a generic term of abuse for anyone
who happened to have brown skin and came from the sub-
continent, whether it was Pakistan itself, India, Sri Lanka, or
Bangladesh.

Whether it was racist or not depends on the context. When our
neighbours were using the term "Paki shop" it wasn't always clear if
they were being prejudiced or not, but when a National Front
member was screaming the word "Paki" at an innocent shopkeeper
there was much less room for ambiguity.

———

THE IRONY BEHIND THIS geographically confused abuse was that
although my parents were Indian, they very nearly ended up in
Pakistan. Had they moved there instead, I probably wouldn't be
telling you this story.

My mother was an asthmatic and the pollution in Mumbai was so bad that she was warned that she'd die if they didn't move. It took little time at all for them to narrow down their choices, finally deciding that they'd either go to Pakistan or London.

These two choices were apparently a 50-50 decision for them, so to help with this process they took a chit, wrote Pakistan on one side and London on the other, then placed it into a copy of the Koran (something you aren't really supposed to do). Whichever way it landed when it fell out of the book was where they decided to go.

In time London won and my mother was finally able to escape the toxic fumes of Mumbai, only to end up in the most polluted part of the UK, in a one-bedroom flat above a shop on Cannon Street Road between Whitechapel and Stepney.

I nearly didn't make it all. I was born in Bradford, six and a half weeks premature, to a woman of Punjabi origin whose family had so objected to the man who fathered me that they forced her to give me up for adoption. Even though I know almost nothing about either of them, I've frequently thought about what must have happened... the best case scenario is that I was the product of an affair. At worst, I suspect that my biological mother may have been raped and that I was discarded as a result of the shame that the family imagined had been wrought upon them.

The couple who adopted me had, by then, suffered through their own ordeal — my adoptive mother, having miscarried twice, fell into an ever-deepening spiral of depression. While adoption might have been an obvious remedy for their situation, culturally, for a Muslim family it was a major taboo. However, a family friend — a doctor — told them about a boy in an incubator who was so small that he could fit in one of their hands. Upon hearing this they were instantly won over, persuaded, in part, by the idea of having a male child.

For the first three or four years of my life there was no maternal bond. The pictures that my father took during this time, in what I think was an attempt to make us closer, show her devoid of any smile and more than likely depressed. It's possible, even probable, that the emotional distance between the two of us had a damaging long-term impact on my development.

School didn't bring much in the way of relief. I went to the Sir John Cass primary school in Aldgate East, which at the time was predominantly white. It was there where I was bullied, with one incident in particular sticking in my mind. A hefty-looking black or Asian girl (I forget which, but be that as it may, she was someone who should have understood my situation) ripped the bobble off a hat I was wearing. As she and several others started tossing it around to one another I started crying from the sense of powerless humiliation that it brought up in me.

––––––––––

There's probably more mythology surrounding this part of London than any other part of Britain, the BBC TV series *Eastenders* being a contributor to this mythology in thrice weekly instalments. One of its first characters, the fruit and veg seller Pete Beale, once proudly described London as "ver greatest city in ver world."

Given that he'd never ventured further from the fictional centre of Walford than Nine Elms, a distance of roughly 15 km (or just less than 10 miles), this was some statement for him to make.

If you walked due north from our family shop on Cannon Street Road, within a mile you'd reach the family home of Charles Kray, father of Reggie and Ronnie (Britain's foremost perpetrators of organised crime on London's East End during the 1950s and 1960s), and a man who went into hiding to avoid active service in World War Two.

The entire area is covered with an overabundance of landmarks for anyone who happens to be fascinated by his sons' "business" interests. The snooker club where they ran their protection rackets was a mile to the east on Eric Street. On your way there you can still drink at The Blind Beggar pub on Whitechapel Road, where Ronnie shot and killed George Cornell (an English criminal and member of the Richardson Gang), allegedly because he'd called him a "fat poof."

With a certain symmetry, Reggie would later end up in Maidstone prison, half a mile from my present family home.

Yet, compared to the area's undisputed criminal mastermind, the Krays were amateurs who were eventually caught. But thanks to the possibly deliberate incompetence of the Victorian police, Jack The Ripper never was, which spawned an industry that thrives to this day.

A few hundred yards from where I went to school, the third of his probable victims, Elizabeth Stride, was murdered. A tri-lingual sex-worker who was originally from Sweden, Stride was one whom, to put it mildly, didn't have much luck with men.

Some time around midnight on September 29, 1888, she was slashed across the neck by a man assumed to be her client. Perhaps disturbed by a passerby, her killer fled before he had the chance to mutilate her corpse to the same degree as his other victims. As such, there's an element of doubt about whether she was actually killed by "Saucy Jack" or some other random, woman-hating psychopath who just happened to be loitering within walking distance of where another sex-worker, Catherine Eddowes, was killed within the next two hours — all just a mile to the west in Mitre Square. The Ripper had a bit more time to work on Eddowes, removing her intestines and draping them over her shoulder.

Today, competing companies offer "Premium Ripper Tours" around the streets from where I grew up. Here's a sample of some of their advertising literature:

"The facts and fictions of the Jack the Ripper case continue to fascinate millions of people around the world. No trip to London is complete without taking part in a free Jack the Ripper tour.

We here at Free Tours By Foot are proud to offer the best alternative Jack the Ripper tour in London. We were the first company to offer free Jack the Ripper tours, and we like to provide our guests with an in depth look at the case. We don't rely on cheesy props or 'spooky' sound effects – this is a tour for the true crime buff and the history junkie alike."

Such an outlook is effectively making death a means of entertainment. In such a setting, the ripper's brutality and misogyny, along with his anti-semitism (there's a long history of racism in the East End) are set aside, the punters (customers) essentially regarding the tours as a bit of a laugh — the real-life victims being so far removed from reality that they may as well be characters from a novel.

One of the explanations for the failure to catch the ripper was that it was a deliberate cover-up. The establishment knew who he was and in a panic had decided they couldn't afford to expose him — and by extension themselves. My own subsequent experiences with the authorities' reluctance to pursue their own suggest that this theory is horrifyingly plausible.

Absorbing mythology like this doesn't do one any good. Later, with my faculties impaired by an addiction to mind-altering substances, I'd harbour fantasies of being some kind of gangster.

———

Once we moved to the relative suburbia of Gants Hill, things improved overall. I felt like a millionaire in our new house. It felt like we were finally getting away from National Front (the far-right, fascist, and racist, political party in the UK), even if we weren't completely isolated from racial bullying and harassment.

On a trip to Hainault Park I saw a group of white men, all of whom had tattoos of what looked like an ancient Hindu symbol, like a cross with feet. Briefly I wondered why a group of white men would by interested in Hindu culture, until I realised that they were the kind of people we'd now call "gammon" (or pigs) and that the symbol they'd emblazoned on their bodies was the swastika. From then on we tended to steer clear of Hainault Park.

Over time my relationship with my adoptive mother went from being rather distant and emotionally disconnected to one that was extremely close. In fact, it was so close that I found myself not wanting to be away from her. When this happened, I found that I dearly loved her. Although I actually never kissed her, she never kissed me either... something that I found to be quite odd. In contrast, my dad kissed me excessively, perhaps trying to compensate for my mum's not doing so.

I was finally able to get emotionally close enough to her that I would confide with her all of my issues — and somehow she would resolve them.

At one point I became fixated on the English football team Tottenham Hotspur. It'd be nice to say that supporting England gave me similarly unambiguous feelings, but there would always be an undertone of danger when the national team would play any big game. As long as England were winning, everyone was happy, myself included. The problem was they hadn't won anything since 1966 and despite having plenty of practise at dealing with defeat, the fans and supporters weren't very good at doing so. The pattern was always the same; flag-waving, face-painted optimism during the build-up to a tournament and the group stages (along with box-ticking messages of tolerance, diversity, and inclusion) that were suddenly rendered meaningless as soon as they'd exit the competition.

I learned to steer clear of public places when England were playing during the business end of either a World Cup or a European

Championship. If they won it was fine to go out where you'd get swept along with the general euphoria. However, if — or more accurately when — they lost, a minority would need an outlet for their rage (with anyone who looked slightly different from them being a potential target). Needless to say, having brown skin put me at risk. I'd learned to read the warning signs and as a result I'd become reasonably adept at avoiding trouble. However, not everyone was as lucky. After England lost to Germany on penalties in Euro '96, a Russian language student was murdered by a "fan" in a sickening act of violence.

I never felt conflicted in my support of Tottenham. Every one of my cousins supported Manchester United, Liverpool, or Arsenal, while the local team was West Ham. However, when I saw Glenn Hoddle on The Big Match, I was smitten.

With his long hair and a shirt that was never tucked in, Hoddle had a swagger and a certain look about him that said 'style'. It was for this reason that, at the time, supporting Tottenham was a joy. There were FA Cup final wins in 1981 and 1982, a UEFA Cup win over Anderlecht on penalties in 1984, as well as some serious title challenges of the kind that we wouldn't mount for another three decades.

My love for Tottenham was both uncomplicated and unconditional — it was one of the most diverse boroughs in the UK where no one cared where you came from or what you looked like. As an example, while I was raised a Muslim, I also happened to be devoted to a team that had been historically associated with the Jewish Community. In what they thought would be an insult, rival fans called us "yids." However, we reclaimed the word and called ourselves the Yid Army — the irony behind this being that we were white, black, Jewish, Muslim, young and old, yet all unifying behind *our team*.

While Liverpool were always on another level, Tottenham were more than a match for Arsenal and Man Utd, and if anyone ever questioned them I'd take it personally... perhaps too personally.

On one occasion, a cousin who was two or three years my junior said that he thought Tottenham were "shit." Hearing this, I slammed his head against a radiator. Seeing this, my Dad (feeling that he had to do something), slapped me in front of the entire family.

Suddenly the feeling of humiliation and powerlessness that I'd felt at primary school returned, and as it did I started to howl. This wasn't unusual. I once lay on the floor of the Gants Hill co-op, screaming for no obvious reason.

Again, for no obvious reason, I once pushed my mum down the stairs. I suspected she was pretending to be unconscious once she'd reached the bottom, but I when I put a finger up her nose to see if she was breathing, she didn't move. At this point I rang 999, which I think was what she wanted and which also seemed like a sensible precaution.

From the above instances, I've reached one of two conclusions — either, I may have had what is now called ADHD, or perhaps I was just a little shit.

———

MY BEST FRIEND IN Gants Hill was "Uncle" Ron, our elderly next door neighbour. Ron had been in the forces and, given his age, I imagine that he'd probably served during World War Two. A balding man of around 5'8" who wore glasses, he had thick black arms and habitually wore a shirt and tie, as men of that era often did, regardless of how uncomfortable it made them feel.

"Uncle" Ron read to me, taught me how to play chess, and — on only one occasion — put his hands down my trousers.

Can you define a man by one act? If so, you'd have to class Ron as a paedophile, even though he never did it again. When I asked him what the hell he was doing he stopped immediately. When I said I was going to tell my parents the colour drained from his face.

When I saw how ashamed he was I told him that I was only joking… and it never happened again.

Our friendship was unaffected. Later I would visit Ron when he was terminally ill with cancer and coughing up blood. While his fate was death, mine was the English boarding school system.

To be honest with you, I'm not sure which was worse.

2

PIERREPONT

According to a survey in the Financial Times, shortly before it closed in 1993, Pierrepont School in Surrey was ranked in the bottom five "public" schools in the country. With tuition and fees of £2523 per term for boarders, it boasted of its strong Combined Cadet Force and said that any pupils who were caught smoking cannabis "risked expulsion."

On the day I was taken to Pierrepont, I cried, and cried again when I left seven years later (although for different reasons). By that stage I'd become like a captive who'd fallen in love with his jailers, or the French revolutionary prisoner who begged to be let back in his cell after his release.

Pierrepont was a living hell, a battery farm of child abuse where cruelty wasn't just a by-product of the way the school was run, it *was* the way the school was run. Parents were effectively paying thousands of pounds a year to have their children traumatised for life. Due to the mafia-like 'Code of Omerta' (which held that reporting abuse was somehow worse than inflicting it), *the abusers got away with it.*

Escaping from Pierrepont should have felt like a liberation, but when the moment finally came I had no idea how I was going to cope on the outside. And for a long time I simply didn't.

———

SET ON AN ESTATE in the rolling Surrey countryside, Pierrepont was a vast, mock-tudor mansion in the village of Frensham, around a mile to the south of Farnham.

If you were looking for the embodiment of a mythical idea of England, this was it — a "public" school on the North Downs, on a hilltop at the end of a driveway that was so long that you needed to make several gear changes before you'd reach the actual building.

With massive wooden doors as its entrance, an oak-panelled reception area, and a vast dining hall, it resembled something out of Hogwarts.

As all fee-paying schools do, Pierrepont had a motto that was written in Latin to impress the prospective punters.

A posse ad esse; (From possibility to actuality)

This motto was something that applied in multiple ways. For one, the possibility that life at Pierrepont was something that I'd suspected before I arrived, while the actuality was significantly worse.

It's easy to see why parents who aspire to a higher life still fall for this kind of thing. Having a child at boarding school was, and still is, seen as a reflection of status — especially for an Indian family making its way in the so-called 'mother country'. The grand scale of such an edifice — with its stained glass windows, ornate carvings and door handles, along with it's giant wooden beams — all eliciting the sense of awe similar to that of being in a cathedral.

Yet sadly enough, they were not around when the myth that they bought into collided with the reality before them — that residential schools not only suffer from almost all of the same problems associated with state schools, they also magnify them. A child who experiences bullying at a comprehensive (a government run school) at least gets to go home to his or her parents every afternoon. At Pierrepont there was no respite.

———————

ON MY FIRST DAY driving down from Gants Hill with my parents, I didn't really understand how being away from them for the first time in my life would impact me.

I can't really blame them for their decision to send me there as boarding school was just something that parents of Indian families did. In fact, in India it was seen as the best way to instil discipline whilst maximising academic achievement. In reality, anything that I achieved happened in spite of being sent into an environment where discipline was a euphemism for sadism, that, more often than not, was accompanied by a sexual undercurrent.

If my parents would have had any idea with regards to what awaited me, I'm sure they would have kept me at home. Yet instead they seemed quite proud that a school had agreed to take several thousand pounds of their hard-earned money. Dressing me in an uncomfortable, ill-fitting, dark blue suit (and combing my greasy hair), little did they realise that they were trussing me up like a lamb about to be sent to an abattoir.

Adding insult to injury, the maroon brief case with two combination locks that they'd given me, with all the best of intentions, had instantly transformed me into a "briefcase wanker." In hindsight it was obvious that something was wrong.

As we drove down from Gants Hill my father was in tears. Whilst my mother was staying strong, my stomach was churning as I was in the midst of a full-blown panic attack, completely oblivious to what was about to hit me.

———————

After Pierrepont School closed in 1993, the site was bought by a company called Ellel Ministries, which describes it as:

> "… a beautiful 35-acre estate in the heart of the Surrey countryside that has been set apart by God to be a place of healing and discipleship for His people. It provides the perfect atmosphere for you to get away from the 'busy-ness' of life, and to meet with God as you enjoy His creation."

Ellel offer "healing retreats" for Christians and their promotional videos show ecstatic-looking converts as they listen to preachers, play Jesus-approved rock music, and are bathed in the cleansing waters of the sacred swimming pool — the irony not be lost on its former inmates. A facebook group called "I Survived Pierrepont School" has over 400 members, most of whom will more than likely be wondering if the place was exorcised before the Lord moved in.

———————

PIERREPONT'S MOST FAMOUS ALUMNI are the England rugby legend Jonny Wilkinson and the actor Sean Pertwee, both of whom seem to have emerged from the experience relatively unscathed. However, there's also a family connection to Robert Baden-Powell, the founder of the Boy Scout movement — and a man with a far more chequered reputation.

In his diary, Baden-Powell once wrote that he, "Lay up all day. Read Mein Kampf. A wonderful book, with good ideas on education, health, propaganda, organisation, etc." This was in 1939, by which time he'd become friendly with Joachim von Ribbentrop, the German ambassador to the UK with whom he'd discussed the idea of sending British scouts to Germany on cultural exchanges with the Hitler Youth.

His apologists claim his flirtation with the Nazi movement was born of naivety accompanied by a fierce hatred of communism. This is at least possible as the innuendo in the title of his book "Scouting For Boys" seems to have been obvious to everyone but the author.

There's also a theory that Baden-Powell was a repressed homosexual. True or not, there was nothing repressed about the homosexuality of some of his apostles at Pierrepont — nor were they shy about using the language of the far right as their every day "banter."

To my peers I was known as the "fat, greasy Paki." Of my new dorm mates, Dok, an African boy, was called 'nigger', 'coon', and 'kaffir'. Paul was short, ergo he was called 'midget'. 'D' was called 'Ram' as it was a shortened version of his surname, while Far was called 'Al-Nas', again after his surname (although he was also known as 'nipples' because of his female-like nipples). Peter was called 'eggy' as he had a egg-shaped head and was posh, while Simon was called 'castrate' as he still had a high-pitched voice. Julian was called "aeroplane nose," as he had a pointed nose, and later became known as "bummer" after he'd become the house master's pet.

The hangover from imperial times was also reflected in the names of the three boarding houses — Trafalgar, Agincourt, and Waterloo — where I was housed along with the seven other new boys, six white kids, Ebiye, and me. As all of them wore jeans and t-shirts, my suit invited even more derision, thus ratcheting up an already deep resentment of my parents.

For the equivalent of well over £2,000 a term, we were given bunk beds and I was grateful for the small mercy of being given a lower bunk. My father's parting gift was a trunk full of confectionary, courtesy of my uncle's cash and carry business, that was was locked and placed next to my bed. However, once my parents had left reality set in for the first time.

That first night I slept in my clothes whilst most of the other kids were enjoying themselves and insulting different races. I cried for what seemed to be all night until I feel asleep, only to be awakened by a loud, continuous bell at 7 AM, which both frightened me and made me start to cry... again. This bell would go off every morning *for the next six years*.

As a result, I didn't want to be there. I felt hopeless and alone. I already hated it... I wanted to leave.

———

I TRIED TO TAKE stock of my new surroundings. Our dorm had polished wooden floor boards, a big long table in the middle, and small framed photos all around the room of previous Waterloo students going all the way back to 1947. Along with all this was a long window overlooking the rugby pitch and tennis courts.

As first formers (first year students) we had to wake up before everyone else. To make sure we didn't lie in, the duty house officer, who was in the fifth form (their fifth year at Pierrepont), would slam our door, giving us our cue to run to the other side of the landing where the wash basins were. We also had to share two urinals with just one main toilet in a separate room.

There were six dorms on the landing with four separate rooms where the house captain, vice house captain, and another prefect resided. As we had a shower rota (rotation, or schedule) which was Tuesday and Thursday nights, the boys used to fill up the sinks with water and dip their heads in them to wet their hair, which everyone did to stop their hair from sticking straight up.

My first full day was a Sunday. All of the Christian boarders had to attend chapel in the main hall, which provided a rare case of the non-Christian boys, like myself, being envied because we got to stay in the library.

The first official day of term was Monday and the morning bell signalled a race to the wash basins before we put on our uniforms for the first time — a white shirt and black blazer with the "a posse ad esse" motto signalling that the possibility of this becoming a nightmare was an actuality.

We queued for the buffet breakfast served by some kitchen assistants who didn't bother masking their resentment of us, presumably because they thought being incarcerated away from your parents was something to envy. From there we went to assembly in the main school building.

The were around 250 pupils in total. We all stood in pairs in our houses and the headmaster walked in, followed by all of his teachers who stood in a line in front of us. If he'd been an honest man his opening words would have been:

> "Welcome to hell. For the next seven years you will be abused in every way imaginable. By the time you leave here, we hope to have scarred you for life and inflicted enough physical and emotional damage to ensure that you spend the rest of your days trying to come to terms with what we've done."

He wasn't an honest man.

———

FRIEDRICH NIETZSCHE ONCE SAID, "That which does not kill us, makes us stronger."

It was bollocks when he wrote it (during an era of cholera, scurvy, and smallpox) and it's bollocks now. Despite this, it has been used to justify all manner of crimes ever since, including those inflicted by the fourth formers at Pierrepont, who decided that the new boys needed to be 'toughened up'.

The initial ceremony at Pierrepont was simple. The fourth formers punched us, not because they were sadists, but because, as they said, they wanted to make us stronger (while it's doubtful, they may even have believed it). In the first week they set the tone for the next seven years by coming to our dorm, forcing the eight of us to stand up, then punching us. When they'd had enough of that they'd get us to punch each other. I used to hold back in the hope that my new room mates would reciprocate, but they never did.

The violence never stopped. Sometimes it was random and spontaneous, while at others it was organised. There was one game in particular called "the cunt" which involved everyone taking a card from a pack. Whoever was left holding the Jack was given "raps" — to wit, their arm was held in place while everyone else took it in turns to hit them on top of their hand with the cards. This might not have been too bad if it had just been a single hit, but it never was. If you were "the cunt" your hand would be smashed repeatedly.

- First the skin would break.
- Then blood would be drawn.
- Then it would start to flow.

Finally, when they were about to break through to the bone, they might finally decide that "the cunt" had had enough.

There was no choice in the matter… if you refused to play they'd beat you anyway. So if you took part willingly you stood a far better chance of avoiding the assault, although sooner or later it happened to everyone.

At other times someone would be randomly selected for a beating, something that usually followed a pattern. There would be two targets, one of whom would be the hard man who'd take absolutely everything that was thrown at him and fight back. The soft target would pretend that one of the blows had hurt him far more than it actually had. Now having done what they'd wanted, the mob would be temporarily satisfied with the hurt that they thought they'd inflicted and everything would calm down… at least for a while.

The one golden rule was to never hit someone in the face, because that might attract the wrong kind of attention. Instead, the solar plexus was a popular target because it winded the victim. Dead arms and legs were also common, where one particular spot on a limb would be repeatedly punched until the limb ceased to function, and the attackers were happy.

All of this treatment resulted in multiple bruises, many visible, whilst many others remained hidden from view. When I did see my parents they'd ask where all the bruises had come from and I'd tell them it was from playing rugby, which in itself might be regarded as a form of organised sado-masochistic activity.

This, therefore, was the reality for the average 11-year-old at Pierrepont — regular beatings, endemic verbal abuse, and no system of redress. If you're wondering how we coped with such delinquency and degradation, the answer is that over the long term, not everyone did. However, some of us did our best to adapt and work out our own survival strategies.

Mine was alcohol.

———————

GETTING ALCOHOL, EVEN AT the age of 11, was almost ridiculously easy. On Saturdays we were allowed to sign out of the school and catch a bus to Farnham Town centre. On my very first weekend I went there with Midget and another friend. Upon our arrival, we immediately made our way to a supermarket where we asked a man, who couldn't have been much older than 19, if he'd buy us some booze.

Even at that age my friends had been exposed to alcohol, having been allowed a sip or two of wine or beer by their parents on special occasions like Christmas. However, as a child of Muslim parents I was a complete virgin. While they, sensibly enough, made it a point to ask for cider (with an alcoholic content of around 4.5 percent), I asked for vodka, which was approximately nine times stronger.

Leaving the market, we took our drink to the nearest park. While the first swig made me feel queasy, I fought through it then tried it again. However, this time I liked it — I liked the burning feeling inside, along with the power and sense of invincibility that it gave me. In fact, I liked it so much that I drank the entire bottle, around three-quarters of a litre, in about ten gulps.

Thinking that I was Superman, I immediately set off running as fast as I could until I smashed into a wall between a pub and a Chinese takeaway opposite Farnham Station. The impact was the last thing I remembered before passing out. For the next nine hours of my life I've been forced to rely on the memories of my friends.

They tell me that they had to carry me to the taxi rank at Farnham Station, where they bundled me in to a cab after promising the driver they'd pay £20 if I was sick.

Fortunately for them, during the short journey back to Pierrepont I managed to avoid throwing up, and was still comatose when my friends saw the headmaster coming towards them on the driveway. It was at this point when they dropped me and ran.

Unfortunately for him, when the headmaster picked me up I vomited all over him, to the hilarity of what was now a fairly large audience as the word had already got 'round that the new boy had gotten drunk, and passed out, on vodka.

I was subsequently taken to Aldershot hospital and put in an induced coma while my stomach was pumped. Around nine hours later I was awake again, spending the afternoon in the matron's quarters, supposedly under observation, before I went back to my dorm. Somewhat incredibly I was back at school the following day. While I was still somewhat fragile, the incident had made my name. From then on I was "the kid who puked on the headmaster."

The following day, by an accident of fate my legend was sealed when I was scheduled to give a talk with another pupil during assembly. On the Sunday night I'd decided I didn't want to talk about the subject we'd originally researched. Instead I wanted to talk about alcoholism.

Even though I may have been useless as a student, I never lacked for confidence. In front of the entire school I stood up and delivered a sermon on the demons of drinking, to the stifled laughter of 250 pupils — and the piss-boiling fury of the headmaster.

When I'd finished he simply said, "I want Buxy in my office, *now.*"

In the office we came to an agreement that the incident would never be mentioned again and that my parents would not be informed. To my 11-year-old self this seemed like a great deal as the last thing I wanted was to tell my mum and dad what had actually happened — although I realised it wasn't a conversation they'd be particularly keen on having either. It was only in hindsight that I finally realised that I'd been conned.

Whilst the headmaster might well have been angry, such an emotion would have almost certainly been far outweighed by fear because an *11-year-old boy in his care had been hospitalised and could have easily died.* Such a revelation would have easily left him open to charges of negligence, and possibly manslaughter. If he wasn't shitting himself about a ruined reputation, the end of his career, and a possible spell in jail, he should have been.

However, we thought we'd got lucky and that this was a win–win situation. (Only later did I realise that if I had told my parents what had happened they might have pulled me out of school.) A week after I'd nearly killed myself, I was back in Farnham Park drinking vodka and coke (and building my tolerance to absurd levels for an 11-year-old), while embarking on a lifelong spiral of addiction.

Quite literally, it was the *only way that I could cope.*

————

THE LAYMAN'S PERCEPTION OF the British Public School system is often warped by its portrayals in cinema and literature. Anyone who thinks that the British film, *Another Country,* is an unrealistic caricature of what it was really like being brought up in a boarding school is absolutely right — it's significantly worse than that. *Lord of the Flies* is closer and *Full Metal Jacket* closer still, but with a different accent and less arse sex.

Pierrepont was a university of inhumanity and the curriculum included sexual abuse, physical violence, racism, and the dehumanisation of absolutely everyone you came into contact with. On one level you could argue that at least it wasn't discriminatory. In fact, to use the words of R. Lee Ermey, (the American actor who played the drill sergeant in the film, *Full Metal Jacket*) we were "all equally worthless." If you had a characteristic that deviated in any way from what was considered normal, it would be used to denigrate you — a law that applied to teachers and students alike.

The headmaster was a skinny, rakish man with glasses and short curly hair with a parting, who was called 'Gimp'. However, this was not because he was the Chief Executive of a 'College of Sado-Masochism' (although that would have worked), but because he had one leg that was an inch longer than the other, making him walk with a limp.

Our housemaster, a man who'd fought in the Burmese War, and must have been on the brink of retirement, was called 'Budgie'. Somewhere around the age of 65, he spoke with a deep, distinctive voice, and a part of his lip was constantly raised... this deformity earning him his nickname.

The twenty-something PE teacher was called 'Dishy' because he thought he was God's gift to women, even though he had ginger coloured hair, something that did not look the least bit masculine on him. The physics teacher was called 'Nipper' because he was short. The Chemistry teacher looked like Nanny McPhee and because she was a woman in an almost-exclusively male environment, we inevitably called her 'Fanny'.

Uglier still was 'Plug', the computer studies teacher who was named after a character in the British comic strip *Bash Street Kids* — a man cursed with ears like the handles on the FA Cup and plagued by boils. 'Eyebrows' looked like the British politician Denis Healey. The geography teacher was simply called 'B.O.' because you could smell him from a mile away... and the stench always lingered in his classroom.

The most aggressive of the lot was a Maths teacher called Gorky, who had a ginger, Bobby Charlton-style combover. It was rumoured that he'd once been a goalkeeper for Luton Town's reserves. When he laughed his mouth would open wide, although he never made a sound.

The English footballer Jackie Charlton also had a lookalike amongst the teachers — our pipe-smoking history teacher, an ex-army officer who rocked back and forth when he was teaching and was called simply, "Bah!"

In that era hair replacement therapy was still in its infancy. As a result, our main science teacher, who resembled an inbred minor royal in a period drama, was known as 'Slap Head'.

The real villain, however, turned out to be 'Faggott', another PE teacher who also taught French. He was slightly older and his head always moved at an alarming speed when he spoke. We always had an inkling that he was a bit suspect because he'd shower with us after PE lessons and walk around the changing rooms naked. His real name was Christopher Wells and in 2004 he pled guilty to 39 counts of making indecent images of children while employed as Head of Modern Languages at Sutton Valence School in Kent. He'd spent five years making thousands of pictures and films while covering his tracks until the police finally caught up with him. At his trial the defence said he was of "good character." In keeping with the Code of Omerta, the school declined to comment. They did, however, contact parents to reassure them that none of the Sutton Valence pupils had been pictured.

Every student had an insulting name, too. There was Fat Cunt, Meat Head, Faggott, Thick Fuck, Ginger, Big Tits, Flat Tits, Ugly Bitch, Spotty, Big Eyes, Frog, Pear Drop, Midget, Skinny Fingers, Did, Gook, Nigger, Pig, Skin, Maggot, Hairy, and Chinky.

I was 'Fat Brown Hairy Paki', with big eyes and a pear-drop shaped head. When I was younger my arm had been badly broken during a bad fall in the park… a clean break that only the skin seemed to be holding together. Unfortunately, it didn't heal properly and as a result you can imagine how sympathetically this kind of ab-normality was treated in such an unforgiving environment.

For the following six years this was the norm. So was the daily bullying, humiliation, physical abuse, and even, at times, torture.

Every single day pupils from the fourth-form upwards would beat us. It was almost as if to do so was their birthright. They'd survived the early years and now it was their turn to "teach us a thing or two about life" by finding out how much we could take. However, it was done in such a scientific manner that you almost had to admire it — they'd worked out how to inflict just enough damage to leave you crying and limping without ever going quite far enough to break a bone and thus force hospitalisation.

One of the house officers, who wore a white, Michael Jackson-style glove, was particularly sadistic. He would enter the dorm without warning to run his fingers along the tops of the framed photos and mirrors. If he found a speck of dirt on any of them, he'd hit our knees with a baseball bat, again with just enough force to wound, but not to maim.

The "Wedgie" was another punishment of choice. Once I was suspended from my 'y-fronts' (my underwear) by a hook out of the dorm window, about 50 feet above the ground. I don't doubt that I would have died if either the material or the wood would have snapped. Nor do I doubt that if I had, the perpetrators would only have cared because of the punishment they would have due.

We also veered a bit into bestiality. One boy, now a presenter and journalist with the BBC, was the main ringleader. He'd organise a posse to strip me naked and hold me down while a grass snake was placed on my penis. The rule here was that if you screamed you'd also be beaten... and the louder the scream, the bigger the beating.

I don't know if I was luckier or unluckier than the boy I saw stripped at 3 AM with a vacuum cleaner attached to his penis. The prefect just said, "Welcome to your first blow-job," while I kept quiet and prayed that I wouldn't be next.

And once I was called into seniors study and forced to play Russian roulette. There were four of us in the prefects room (myself and three others) with a gun that had a big wooden butt. To this day I've no idea if it was loaded or not. The fact that no one was killed (that I know of) suggests that it probably wasn't. Yet, as a boy surrounded by his peers who thought nothing of holding their fellow classmates out of top floor windows, suspended only by their underwear, it was impossible to be sure.

Operating through the Code of Omerta, Pierrepont was like a mini-mafia state. The culture was one in which you didn't "grass" (snitch) on anyone... and one in which people went along with anything that happened because they were too cowed to do anything else. In Pierrepont, as in Sicily, reporting a crime was supposedly worse than committing one. That was why nothing ever changed. When I went home to see my parents, I explained my bruises by saying I'd been playing rugby, a sport that evolved from public schoolboys indulging in rugged, consensual physical contact. The only difference between scrumming, rucking, mauling, and life in a Pierrepont dorm, was that at least on the rugby field a referee would intervene every now and again.

———————

UNFORTUNATELY, MY NEAR DEATH experience with alcohol didn't put me off. By the age of 11 I was addicted. At 12 my tolerance levels were so high that I began mixing my drinks. Snakebite was a cocktail of lager, cider, and blackcurrant that hardcore drinkers who were two or three times my age considered to be lethal. Yet for me it felt like Camomile tea… so I started to add vodka to it.

Drinking was the only way I could cope. When I drank I forgot about the beatings. I stopped worrying about the seniors who'd throw me in the stinging nettles, or "shaverape" me by taking a razor to my face (even though my parents had told me not to start shaving until I was 16 because they were worried about regrowth).

When I drank I could shut out the constant racial abuse, and alcohol gave me the confidence to do all of the crazy things that made me popular. With my peers at least, I'd developed a reputation as someone you didn't mess with — it helped that Midget, my best friend, was a real fighter. However, that didn't stop the seniors from beating me, even though in my year group, the violence abated and I became an entertainer, the class clown who would flick ink at Fanny when her back was turned.

Like everyone else at Pierrepont, I still lived with the constant fear that I was about to have the shit kicked out of me. You might be thinking that from this point on things could only get better, but at the age of 13 I made one of the biggest mistakes of my life.

I joined the army.

3

C. C. F.

The Combined Cadet Force is run by the Ministry of Defence and is popular with a certain kind of school. It advertises itself as an organisation that,

> "offers young people aged 12 to 18 a range of challenging, exciting, adventurous, and educational activities."

Their stated aim is to "enable the development of personal responsibility, leadership, and self-discipline."

What they don't tell you is that your more psychotic peers will try to do this by calling you a "Paki bastard," and sticking blunt instruments in your arse. At Pierrepont the army was seen as the best service to join, so I signed up and entered an even deeper dimension of hades.

Army recruitment officers are liars. They always have been and they've always had to be. If they told recruits the truth, which is that any soldier who sees combat stands a real chance of getting either seriously injured or killed, no one would join. Nor do they tell you that after a spell with the CCF, death might not seem like a bad option.

Instead they tell you it's chance for you to "be the best."

CCF was physical and mental torture. Loaded with back packs and rifles, we were told to tackle assault courses and screamed at all the way round. My arm made the course even more demanding than it would have been under normal circumstances. If I couldn't perform the task I was set, I was told that I'd let my squad down. This meant they would get punished by the instructors, while I was left untouched.

The instructors did this in the full knowledge that the rest of the squad would extract their revenge later on by collectively beating me. It was exactly like the scene in *Full Metal Jacket* when Private Pile is pinned to his bunk and hit by every member of his group, the difference being that while they were grown adults, I was only 13 years old.

Let's call this what it was — institutional child abuse — and it would only get worse.

————

THE SELF-HELP INDUSTRY is full of charlatans who'll parrot mantras like "never quit." Quitting anything other than smoking or alcohol is considered to be morally suspect — quitting the army is borderline treason. This culture explains why I, as a 13-year-old boy, decided to stick with the CCF and take a trip to Germany where we were on camp with the The Queen's Own *Hussars Tank Regiment*. It wasn't compulsory, but we were effectively told that if we wanted to stand any chance of rising to the rank of lance corporal, we'd need to go. So I went.

Somehow it was even worse than Pierrepont, which I didn't think was possible. We fetched up in a camp somewhere near the

French border, in a base that had been set up after a war that was supposed to have defeated fascism, only to find that it was alive and well in the British Army.

I got my first taste of how enlightened the British forces on the Rhine were when we played a football match and grown men stood on the sidelines, shouting "get the Paki bastard" at me. Squaddies would rugby tackle me when the ball was on the other side of the pitch. You can imagine how easily Britain conquered a third of the globe if their ancestors could muster the same contempt for their enemies as these men had for a 13-year-old British Asian boy.

Things got worse when we went on exercises. I was given the chance to drive an APC Ambulance tank, which is something that probably excites a certain kind of schoolboy, but which is a different proposition when you're 13 years old and you're suddenly told you're going to be responsible for handling two tonnes of metal.

The instructors weren't that effective at teaching us either, but when I accidentally buried the barrel the attitude was not: "everyone makes mistakes, it's the only way to learn." The reaction wouldn't have been a lot worse if I'd blown up a hospital. They decided to punish me by making me do push ups in dog shit. And when I'd completed them, they thought that I still needed to be beaten, individually, by everyone on the camp.

———

THE LAST NIGHT WITH the regiment was probably one of the worst of my life. To begin, we decided to celebrate what we thought was the end of the trip by drinking sambuca until the early hours of the morning.

After finally going to bed, four seniors came into our room and immediately began to sexually assault the four of us, myself included. One of the seniors, 'Skin', stripped me and started to penetrate me rectally with a brush handle. Opposite me I saw another kid being penetrated in exactly the same way by another senior, but he was doing this so violently that I could see extensive bleeding. Two other seniors abused the others in our group.

It was a sick thing to be a part of, but even though I was one of the victims (as victims most often do), I blamed myself for the abuse. Above all others that I've experienced, this incident has stayed with me for my entire life.

I wonder if Her Majesty has any idea about what was being done in her name. Funnily enough, calling me a Paki bastard, burying my face in dog shit, kicking the living crap out of me, and shoving a blunt instrument up my arse didn't enhance my desire to lay down my life "for Queen and country."

When we got back to school the headmaster had obviously been tipped off concerning what had happened, because he summoned the victims of the tortuous treatment into his office. He was *adamant* that our parents shouldn't be notified as he claimed that this would make us feel even more humiliated.

This, in itself, was child abuse. While the headmaster knew exactly what had happened, he denied us our victimhood along with any chance of justice, merely to save both his reputation along with that of the school. He was complicit and an enabler — a man who had abused his position for far too long… and gotten away with it (as did the perpetrators). One of them finally became an army officer (he clearly enjoyed a taste for it) before moving seamlessly into the police force, where he rose effortlessly up the ranks. Another became an accountant. While I don't know what happened to the rest of them, what I *do* know is that I couldn't even talk about what had happened that night for another 25 years.

———

THE WEIRD THING IS that on my last day at Pierrepont I actually cried. The last two years weren't actually that bad, mainly because by that point most of the serial abusers had left.

However, in spite of this my behaviour hadn't significantly improved. I was still drinking regularly and also continued to be very disruptive in my classes. Myself and another friend, Jimmy, would go into history class with the specific intention of getting kicked out. We'd begin by entering the classroom pushing each other, then both of us would somersault onto our desks. It worked. We'd get thrown out immediately and go to Jimmy's dorm, where we'd smoke cigarettes by his chimney in an effort to hide the smell.

On the rare occasions when I actually put my mind to something, I did reasonably well. I soon won quite a few public speaking competitions, then started to act. I played Ernie in *Ernie's Incredible Hallucinations* by Alan Ayckbourne… and as it was my best performance to date, I celebrated by getting heavily drunk with my friends Midget, Eggy, and the Gooks.

Near the end of my time there my best mate was Jimmy who was in Trafalgar House. I sometimes went with him when he'd go home. On one of these occasions he'd organised a massive party which he called, "The Libido Ball."

I remember my mum calling Jimmy's mum beforehand and asking her to look after me. Jimmy's mum turned round and saw me with a bottle of vodka in my hand and a cigarette between my lips.

"Don't worry, he's fine," she said.

While I was the only non-white at the party, by then that was something I was getting used to. I did get a bit of attention from a couple of girls, but nothing really materialised, more than likely due to my general madness and intoxication.

Life in general might have improved overall towards the end of our time at Pierrepont, yet even after everything that we'd survived, there was one final, tragic act that would hit us right between the eyes. Our friend Chris was one of the nicest, loveliest individuals you could ever meet — and a brilliant rugby player as well — who had serious aspirations of playing for England.

After our History GCSE, Jimmy, Porky, and I were chatting with him on the school grounds as he revved up his 125 CC motorbike. I can remember at the time thinking that it didn't sound too great, but whether or not that caused what happened shortly thereafter, I don't know. He was killed in a head on crash outside Charterhouse School. We were probably the last people he ever spoke to. In a rare moment of humanity, even though we were in the middle of our exams, the school allowed us to attend his funeral.

I HAD ONE FINAL farewell that I wanted to say to the teachers at Pierrepont. One final "fuck you" to the abusers and enablers — the bastards who'd turned a blind eye as the school destroyed our childhoods.

On my last day I recorded a cassette tape of myself cussing every last one of the teachers. When the moment was right, we went to Jimmy's room, put the tape player by the window and cranked up the volume to its maximum possible setting. Then we hit play, left the room, and locked the door behind us.

One last act of revenge against "Fishy" the PE teacher, who'd once strangled me for daring to talk back to him.

One final parting shot at the paedophile Chris Wells for pulling on my sideburns so hard that he made the skin show underneath.

One last tirade at the Headmaster, the Emperor of this child abuse factory, the man who facilitated and covered up sex crimes against the small, terrified children in his care.

And yet when my parents came to pick me up, I cried. Pierrepont was all that I'd known for six years. Maybe I was crying because I thought the abuse was finally over. What I didn't realise was that a past like this isn't something that you can easily escape.

4

ON THE OUTSIDE

While school is supposed to prepare you for adulthood, what I'd found to be true once I left is that Pierrepont had damaged me almost beyond repair.

After six years, and tens of thousands of pounds spent by my parents, I left Pierrepont having passed just three GCSEs (an set of competency exams that one takes in the UK at the age of 16, also known as a General Certificate of Secondary Education) and one of those was for PE, which you only needed a pulse to pass. I got a B in that, a C for English, and a solitary A for English Oral... I'd failed everything else. Having already wasted an astronomical sum of money on my education, my parents now insisted that I should go to another private college and retake my exams.

As a result, I enrolled in the Davies, Laing, and Dick College in Pembroke Square in Notting Hill Gate, right next door to a nursery that Prince William was attending at the time. Studying in London was a huge culture shock for me, because there were other cultures than the white of Pierrepont — and even more shocking was that there was no hint of discrimination or abuse.

Academically, in this new environment I thrived, passing eight GCSEs and getting three As in the process. However, I also became even more proficient at drinking, which, given that I was already an expert, was saying something.

I was very close to my commerce teacher, Judy, a lovely woman from County Cork who eventually became a family friend. She was married to an American body builder who rather sadly passed away a few years later. Since we were both Guns 'n Roses and Tottenham fans, we went to a few matches and concerts together.

I tried my first spliff (a joint that consists of tobacco and marijuana or hash) while I was at DLD… and it absolutely knocked me out. I have no idea how I got home but when I did, my dad thought I was drunk and because of this (and being Muslim) he slapped me. Since I was high, instead of being horrified I started laughing, and this apparent lack of concern on my part made him even more angry. Needless to say, it was a chastening experience, after which I promised myself that I'd never smoke weed again.

Soon I became close to two Armenian bodybuilder brothers who were studying for their A levels at the time, lived in a flat in Bayswater, and drove an S class Mercedes. They were also living the high life, which happened to be a very big attraction for me. Even though I was only 16 at the time, they took me to exclusive night clubs in Central London and got me in to VIP lounges. They also introduced me to films like *Scarface* and *Goodfellas*, which had only just been released.

The lifestyle that was depicted in those films was very seductive to me — as a result I became obsessed with Al Pacino. I wanted to emulate him, so I studied him… reading about his life and watching his films over and over again. It wasn't long before I decided that, like Al, I wanted to become an actor. My only stumbling block to realizing this decision was my parents who wanted me to go to university. Whereas Tony Montana started out in a Cuban refugee camp in Florida, I found myself at Enfield College. While Tony made his way in the world by killing drug dealers and Cuban generals, I took the BTEC National Diploma in Business and Finance.

Enfield College was very multi-cultural with a high percentage of Afro-Caribbean and Turkish students. My best friends there were both girls — one a teetotaling Somalian called 'Ami', and the other, an orphan we called 'Shorty'.

Originally from Mauritius, Shorty had lived in a children's home from a very young age and more likely than not, due to this background she was too emotionally volatile for any one of a succession of boyfriends. (It probably didn't help that she and I were always drinking and smoking weed.) Ami wanted to be more than friends, but at that point I was still shy around girls — another area in which Pierrepont had left me woefully underprepared for life on the outside.

After a while I moved in with an Indian guy whom I'll call 'K'. We got on brilliantly because he was as crazy as I was, but living together was almost a guarantee of mutually assured destruction.

We both loved causing damage — whether it was to properties, cars, or night clubs — but what I liked about 'K' was that he was absolutely fearless... and I knew that I could count on him to have my back. I can clearly remember an incident in a pub in which he was playing pool against some builders who were double our age. When he beat them on the black I cheered, but the next thing I knew was that my head had been put through the window. Rather than call me an ambulance the landlord decided to throw me out, so we went away, got cleaned up, and came back later that night to smash his remaining windows. However, this time we used blunt instruments thrown from a distance as opposed to my head from close range.

'K' lived in Tottenham along with another guy called Dee (and we're still mates today), the three of us bonding over the shared amazement that we'd all lasted as long as we had. We also bonded over weed, smoking a lot of it together. While marijuana on its own isn't likely to kill, it *can* push you down a much more dangerous set of paths.

We'd start by doing silly things like diving into park lakes fully clothed, but when the excitement from that subsided we graduated to more dangerous activities like starting fires. In hindsight, it feels like we were almost sociopathic, because the idea that we might harm someone either didn't occur to or concern us. It wasn't long before 'K' and I became experts at stealing from bags and coats in nightclubs, just for the thrill of it. For the most part, we didn't even make a lot of money out of it, but even when we did we just blew it on drink and drugs. It was fun at the time, but it also stifled us. "K' had talent and I'm sure that if he hadn't been such a loose wire he could've been a successful professional pool or snooker player.

It was around this time that I suffered my second near death experience. Passing my driving test was probably the first meaningful achievement that I'd ever accomplished on my own. However, for whatever reason, I thought that it would be a good idea to celebrate buying my first car by drinking a bottle vodka and then smoking weed. The danger to young drivers is at its highest point just after they've passed their driving test since they no longer have an instructor to stop them from doing something stupid.

Feeling invincible, I drove to Tottenham and was doing 50 mph on the Roundway when I lost control on a sharp bend and ploughed into some railings on the opposite side of the road. It was a minor miracle that no one was coming the other way given how busy that section of road is, but for the second time in my life I needed to have stomach pumped. My dad, it's perhaps needless to say, wasn't too pleased, but by that point he was just relieved that I was alive.

After scraping my diploma, I was accepted at Westminster University where I was supposed to be studying Industrial Systems and Business Management. Instead I took a PhD in the consumption and abuse of alcohol.

As I fell in with a couple of friends from Pierrepont (who I'll call 'Bertie' and 'Big Black'), my drinking escalated. Bertie also had a twin called 'Spik' and as a trio we became inseparable. We would drink, smoke, party, and take drugs, and when that wasn't enough we'd go out with their elder brother — who also happened to be a world champion kick boxer — looking for a fight.

While 'Bertie' and I would be steaming from the booze, and 'Spik' would be stoned out of his mind, they also knew how to kickbox, so we'd wander 'round central London looking for someone to rile. I'd start on someone, knowing that if they reacted my friends would batter them... and invariably they did.

Emboldened by my friendship with a gang of kickboxers, and by now in an almost permanently intoxicated condition, I became a practitioner of some seriously anti-social behaviour. For starters I began to 'pull moonies' *everywhere* including inside theatres. I'd set off fire alarms in five-star hotels and jump out of cabs without paying the fare. While this kind of behavior got me arrested on numerous occasions, I completely failed to learn my lesson.

On one occasion Bertie gambled away all of his money and didn't have anything left to spend on a birthday gift for his dad. Then one of us had a brainwave... more like a brain fade. We headed to Soho and stood outside one of the brothels pretending to be pimps. As soon as a client would hand me the cash, we'd both run. While it wasn't the brightest of ideas, Bertie got to buy his dad a present... and I got to buy more alcohol. We reasoned that if they'd caught us, what were they going to do? Bertie was a kickboxer and because of what they were doing, they were hardly going to call the police.

I only lasted about four months at Westminster University before I was asked to leave due to my practice of disrupting lectures. I was usually utterly arseholed when I'd turn up, so I can't say that I blamed them for doing that. Unfortunately my mum also decided that this was an appropriate time in my life to tell me that I'd been adopted… a revelation that hit me like a jackhammer.

In fact, my whole world stopped. While I'd survived Pierrepont, with all of the abuse and degradation that had caved in my world from the *outside*, now with this revelation my world had caved in from the *inside*. What made it worse was that, apart from me, every other fucker around me somehow seemed to know this. Every whispered conversation between family members — every pitying look that I'd ever received at family gatherings — had suddenly taken on a whole new meaning.

As you might guess, I coped in the only way that I knew how, by leaving the house that night and buying a bottle of vodka, which I downed without a second thought. Afterward, I roamed the streets of London, where I encountered all sorts of different unsavory characters, and finally slept rough on the streets.

Within a few months I was accepted at Middlesex University where I was supposed to study Economics. However, it wasn't long before history would repeat itself. I caused the same level of disruption in lectures. Then for whatever reason, I somehow got a job in the student bar. It goes without saying that this was a huge mistake as I inevitably spent significantly more time drinking and smoking cannabis than I ever invested in my studies.

This was a time when my parents were living in Oakwood, Enfield, in North London… a borough marked by several 'firsts' in the world, and a major step up for my parents. One weekend, when they'd taken a holiday for themselves, I decided that it was time to hold a massive party at my house.

However, this wasn't just going to be *any* party. In fact, it was so big that I'd hired bouncers for the front door. Yet, you couldn't hold a party like this in a neighbourhood like that without attracting the wrong kind of attention. The police turned up and one of the neighbours told my uncle about their visit. When he called me, since I was off my face, I was abusive to him. And being so intoxicated, I didn't even realise who it was when he called.

Eventually, I was kicked out of Middlesex University, too, because I was too busy studying the effects of narcotics to be interested in anything academic... and the next module in my course would be LSD. With another Pierrepont survivor, whom I'll call 'Ace', I dropped some acid... and it wasn't long before the effects kicked in. He was with a girl and when her hands started caressing him the two of them looked like giant spiders, which made me panic, so I smacked them. Then I went upstairs to Ace's room where he had all these photos of female models on the wall — whilst I was tripping, they all seemed to come alive.

I found that I just couldn't handle LSD, which was more than likely good for me. However, a few weeks later I found a drug I was more compatible with... ecstasy. It was *wonderful*. I tried it with Bertie and Spik and, especially with music, the feeling was lovely. By the end of the night Spik and I were at Primrose Hill just talking about our lives. I told him about my adoption and he told me about the separation from his twin brother. It was a profound experience for me. In particular, I easily remember the morning after... when I began to experience the come down how a pint of beer brought back those feelings from the previous night.

Taking these drugs was like an escape from *everything*. I felt free and untouchable. Being high was the only way that I knew how to deal with everything, even though that didn't make me a convert to the idea of peace and love. Occasionally I still liked to dabble with violence, especially when I was accompanied by my Pierrepont mate

'Big Black', who was both. At 6' 5" tall, 'Big Black' was a half Jamaican, half African guy with a shaved head and a baby face that somehow still looked like a menacing threat to those he met.

We were like a double act. At boarding school he had a reputation of being the hard man while I was the joker. We either entertained people, or beat the shit out of them. Some people loved us. I dread to think what the others thought. On one occasion we thought it'd be a good idea to go back to Farnham for a school reunion, but I was wankered before I'd even got out of the station.

It was packed and I hadn't even made it to the concourse when I noticed a group of lads looking at me from the opposite platform. When I drank I thought I was indestructible, especially when I had either kickboxers with me or a 6' 5" brawler. I stupidly jumped on the train tracks, dodged the rails, climbed on to the platform, smacked one of the lads in the face, and then made the possible suicidal return journey to the platform where I'd originally been. By now about six of this lads mates were hurling abuse at me, so I did the same thing back, but this time they were ready for me. When I got to the other side they rushed me and I was getting beaten on the platform. I covered my face and waited for Big Black to arrive, but he wasn't stupid enough to cross the tracks, so I had to wait for him to make his way over via the stairs while their furious blows continued to rain down on me.

One at a time he picked them off. They shat themselves and ran, but Big Black was able to trap one of them and started pounding his face into the platform, hitting him so hard that his face was becoming deformed. Now that I'd been able to get back on my feet, I was kicking him like Robert DeNiro's character in *Goodfellas*, while everyone else on the entire platform watched in silent horror.

In those days there were no CCTV security cameras anywhere, so we just carried on until we heard the police sirens, at which point we legged it and hid in a bush. As we hid for the next 40 minutes, we made up a story just in case we were caught. Then we lit up a spliff and started to laugh about what had just happened, which must have given us a false level of confidence. When we finally decided that the coast was clear we thought it would be a smart move to walk back to the station. Within two minutes four cop cars had us barricaded, then we were handcuffed and taken to the police station... just like a scene from *New Jack City*. The adrenaline was pumping — while I was afraid, I was also excited. For the next two nights we were locked up in separate cells, interviewed separately, then finally released on bail.

Fortunately for us, we both gave the same story, which was that we'd acted in self-defence. The police posted notices around Farnham with our sketches on them asking for any witnesses to come forward. However, none did, possibly out of fear after witnessing what Big Black might do to anyone who did.

When I finally got back to Enfield and told my mother what had happened, she was shocked. Public school had failed — so had two universities. Coming to this realisation, she decided that it was time to ask a higher power for help. With that, she booked me a flight to Mecca... and decided to pray to God.

5

L.A.

Instead of Mecca, God responded to my mother's prayers by sending me to Los Angeles, where I planned to become an actor.

In Quentin Tarantino's 1994 film, *Pulp Fiction*, Uma Thurman's character, Mia Wallace, is the wife of the local gangster. She's also a failed actress and cokehead whose distant claim to fame was that she'd appeared in a pilot for a show called *Fox Force Five*. Since only about a quarter of the pilots that ever get made will become a series, Mia's was one of the three-quarters that didn't. In spite of that, she still got further along in her acting career than I would.

Up to this point, I'd been to the Cannes Film Festival (where I'd made a few industry contacts), and I'd also auditioned at the Lee Strasberg studio in London where I'd done well enough to get accepted for a place at their school in Los Angeles.

On my first day there I was accompanied by Emmett Humphries and Phillipe Rhys, both of whom now have reasonably successful careers in the entertainment industry — first as actors, then also as producers, directors, and voiceover artists. They're both still active in the industry, having done well enough to earn a living without ever quite hitting the big time.

Emmett, who changed his name to Emmett James, later got himself a bit part in Titanic, while Phillipe has been in a number of projects that you've probably seen, like *Doctor Who*, without ever attracting a starring role. While they might not be famous, nine out of ten of people who try to make it in Hollywood fail. In our group the failure rate was one in three, and for reasons that will soon become clear, I was the one who failed.

I didn't get on with Phillipe, whom at the time was calling himself Phillip Chowdry. I thought he was arrogant and obnoxious, so the tension between us bubbled under the surface from the word go. Yet we managed to keep a lid on it for a while and found a beautiful house on North Genesee Avenue, a boulevard lined with palm trees and white, cubic buildings that could have easily been a backstreet in a Mediterranean resort, as Los Angeles has a similar climate. It also had some of the undercurrents that you'd find in less salubrious Mediterranean cities.

On the day that we moved in, the three of us decided to go for a walk along Melrose Avenue. As we made our way down this hip, yet somewhat funky street, a young, hispanic-looking kid came up to me and asked if I had any change. I didn't. I can still remember the shiver of fear that I felt as I noticed the weapon he was carrying in his belt. He couldn't have been more than ten years old and here he was carrying a pistol. Fortunately I took that as fair warning that I needed to be careful while I was in LA.

I developed a morning ritual. Every day I'd get up and go to the Starbucks on Melrose for a muffin, a panini, and a cup of tea. In hindsight I realise that I was doing this because I already felt like the odd one out in the apartment that we'd only just moved into. Things were glacial between Phillipe and I and although they were better with Emmett, I knew that when it came down to it, he would always side with Phillippe.

IF YOU'RE GOING TO make it in LA you need a break. I got the wrong kind. As beautiful as the apartment was, I was already reluctant to spend time there, so instead I'd go for walks around the neighbourhood. On one afternoon I was passing a shop when I saw a tall guy with a distinctive Mancunian (an English Manchester) accent trying to persuade people to go inside. As we got talking, he told me that his name was Richard and that he was originally from Moss Side but had come to L.A. because his sister had married a local.

It's from here when the story gets a bit hazy. He was living with his brother-in-law, but his sister was still in Manchester. As he was soon to be heading back to England, I got his job along with an introduction to his brother-in-law, whose name also happened to be Richard. This would have been confusing enough to deal with when sober, but the second Richard happened to be a crack addict who also smoked PCP and cannibis, so I effectively got lumbered with him. I owed his brother-in-law a favour because he'd got me this job, but now I was alone — due to a falling out that I'd had with Phillippe and Emmett — and I didn't have anyone else.

Richard lived in Compton, a district of South Central L.A. that was infamous to young men of my generation because of the rap group *NWA* and the film director Spike Lee. His brother, Eric, was in the Crips, which was usually described as a "gang" even though in reality it was more of an organised crime syndicate.

The Crips had around 13,000 members who were scattered across the city, making their money through drug trafficking, protection rackets, extortion, burglary, robbery, racketeering, and gambling — activities that had left a trail of blood flowing across the city.

I have to confess that at the time I had a morbid fascination with that kind of lifestyle. I'd seen films like *New Jack City* and *Boys In The Hood*... films that were horrifying and compelling at the same time.

The problem was that such a way of life was incompatible with trying to hold down a job of any kind, let alone the kind of job that you're only doing because you want to pay for acting classes.

Using my charm, along with my English accent, I'd spend the day trying to coax people into this particular shop on Melrose. Oddly enough, it worked. In fact, I was so good at it that the owner of the women's shop next door, a huge Italian with a ponytail that made him look like a porn star, poached me and I started working for him instead.

Now I got into a routine. I'd work, go home, have something to eat, then head to acting classes. I first enrolled at the Lee Strasberg school, but that didn't seem like enough on its own, so I also started going to the Stella Adler Method Acting Studio on Hollywood Boulevard. That wasn't enough either, so I joined Charles Laughton's school as well, partly because he was Al Pacino's mentor.

This wasn't a great mix. Method acting involves subsuming yourself in the character to the point of forgetting that you're a performer. The character's reality becomes your reality and when the character's reality is that of a paranoid junkie like Tony Montana that isn't great for your mental well-being.

On Friday nights I'd get off work and take one of the motorbikes that I'd bought with Phillippe and Emmett over to the Viper Room, a couple of miles away on the Sunset Strip. This was a club that had only been open for around a year, but it had already earned a reputation of infamy.

A few months earlier River Phoenix had stopped there, telling his girlfriend that he wanted to jam with some musicians he knew, and 45 minutes later he was dead. Already "high," according to his girlfriend Samantha Mathis, at some point after going inside he'd also taken heroin. Mathis next saw him being ushered outside, where he began to convulse on the pavement. The "friend" he was with told Mathis to leave him alone because she was spoiling his high.

His death should have been a warning, but I was oblivious to the signs it should have pointed out. To make matters worse, the Viper Room staff either didn't know, or didn't care, what their customers were getting up to. To be allowed entry you had to show your passport to the bouncer at the door, but once you were in it was a dark, seedy place where absolutely anything went... and you could still get off your face. So I did. I'd begin by pre-loading with some crack, then drink heavily, and finally start smoking weed... all while watching an unbelievable jazz-funk and soul show.

Sometime around 1 or 2 AM Richard would pick me up and drive me to the south of the city, where we'd find Latino clubs hidden away along the back streets in buildings that looked like they could easily fall down at any moment. Richard would knock on what looked like a random sheet of corrugated metal that was propped up against the wall of a construction site, but what was in fact the "front entry" to a nightclub.

If the four huge Mexicans behind the door didn't tell you to fuck off, you were then escorted through a warehouse area to a second door... and behind this was the actual club. A passerby would have no idea these underground venues even existed and that was the point. Just like their clientelle, they operated well beyond the outer limits of the law.

On one occasion I witnessed a young couple dancing. I had no idea whether they were married, boyfriend and girlfriend, or just out on a date. Whatever the case, the woman happened to accidentally catch the eye of a local gangster, who was sitting in the corner surrounded by an entourage of sycophants. Catching her gaze, the gangster walked over to her and groped her arse. Seeing this, her date asked him to stop, then walked her to a different part of the club. Nevertheless, the gangster followed them and persisted. Before the man could even open his mouth to protest a second time, at least ten thugs suddenly jumped him and started to kick and punch with such violence that it was obvious to anyone that he was suffering broken bones and worse. In spite of this, the door staff just looked on while the woman was left to scream.

I didn't want to hang around to see what happened next, but rather than leave, Richard and I just went into the next room where we started smoking crack. From there we drove into the Hollywood Hills and parked up at a site right opposite the Hollywood sign, where we smoked primos — spliffs with crack added to the mix — and now I was flying, in a spiritual sense — as by this time I'd entered a different dimension entirely… a dimension where the dangers of attempting to ride a motorbike while high on a cocktail of some of the most potent drugs known to humanity had completely eluded me.

Oddly enough, it was in this incredibly altered state that I decided to ride home. Somehow I miraculously was able to navigate the back streets, finally making my way to Melrose Avenue. It was when I'd nearly reached my apartment that I happened to clip the kerb, and now I was flying in a purely physical sense — something that I can't say that I'd recommend.

I was unconscious for perhaps a couple of minutes before I came to and looked up to see bits of my bike scattered all over the road. I burst into tears because I didn't think I could move, but somehow the drugs and panic had kicked in, the feeling in my limbs returned, and just like Robocop, I suddenly got up. I'd started picking up bits of my bike when the LAPD arrived and asked if I was "all right." Here I was again, grateful for my English accent. My trousers were ripped to shreds and I don't know what I must have looked like, but as soon as they heard me begin to say something they relaxed, made a joke, and left.

In spite of the drugs kicking in, by now I was in excruciating pain. Yet I was so relieved when they went away that I limped back to the apartment and collapsed into bed. The next thing I remember was waking up to find four tall men with slicked back hair, wearing

RayBans, who were all staring at me. Phillippe and Emmett had seen the state of my knees and called for an ambulance. This was the crew.

All I can say is thank God that I had medical insurance. They took me to Cedars-Sinai Hospital on Beverly Boulevard where I was given tests, brain scans, and a physio recovery programme over two days, all of which would have costs me thousands of pounds if I hadn't had cover. It was only later that insult was added to serious injury when I finally discovered that while all this was happening, Pacino and DeNiro were shooting the film *Heat* on the ground floor. I had no idea they were even there, let alone that I'd missed the chance to see what would become one of the greatest crime thrillers of all time being made.

Having missed one chance to meet my idol, just a few days later I also missed another. As my limbs healed and my bike was put back together, I decided that I'd carry on almost as exactly as I had before, with only a slight change to my lifestyle. While this would have been a good time for me to lay off the drugs and concentrate on my acting classes, instead (true to form) I concentrated on the drugs and laid off the acting classes. This meant that when Pacino turned up at Charles Laughton's school to film another part of *Heat*, I wasn't there. After the fact I was told that he took the entire class out for breakfast.

Instead of acting in a gangster movie, I was living in one… and living dangerously, I might add. When Richard and I went out looking for "sherm" (cigarettes that have been pre-soaked in angel dust), the only thing that stopped the dealer from shooting us was the state of Richard's thumb. He'd smoked so much crack that the skin on his thumb had burned away — it was only this detail that convinced the dealer that we weren't undercover cops.

Sherm was a very different narcotic experience. On one occasion when I smoked it, I was on Santa Monica beach and found myself completely unable to either talk or walk. The weird thing was that there was no comedown to it, but it altered your perception of time so drastically that I thought 20 minutes had gone by when, in fact, several hours had elapsed. Even though I was taking almost everything else, I never took that again.

Overall, I was in LA for around a year and a half. At one point I was smoking five rocks per day, along with an eighth of cannibis, or 'mota' (a street term for 'Thai stick'), which I'd buy from the Mexicans downtown. I was also using speed and endo weed (at the time, an LA slang term for weed grown indoors) and washing it all down with nearly a fifth of vodka every day. This went about as well as you might expect. At one point I remember looking in a mirror and seeing that my face was so blistered and distorted that I thought I was the Elephant Man. To this day I can't tell you if those blisters were real, or just a figment of my imagination. Although when I rang my parents and told them about this, they told me to go to a doctor. Once I did, the blisters cleared up, so I imagine that they must have been real.

Even though I was falling to bits, I was still able to conjure up one final LA performance to coincide with the night of the 1994 Academy Awards. My gatecrashing skills had always been Oscar-worthy and I managed to get myself, Phillippe, and Emmett into a post-ceremony party. Michael J Fox was there, as was Jeremy Irons, who frankly, in my opinion, came across as rude. Uma Thurman was in tears because she'd been nominated for the Best Supporting Actress award and had lost out to Dianne Wiest for Woody Allen's film *Bullets Over Broadway*. Jack Nicholson, as I understand it, was in the toilets snorting cocaine.

Such a crazy experience was entirely befitting of my time in L.A. However, by this point in the evening I was too ill to appreciate it, and realising this, I left early.

My acting career was going nowhere, I'd lost my job because I was high all the time, and the money that my parents had given me was about to run out.

In this weakened state, Richard and I decided that we had one last option. We drove through the desert to Las Vegas where I intended to gamble my way into a fortune. At one point I was $10,000 dollars up, but by that stage, to quote Harvey Keitel in *From Dusk Till Dawn*, "I was such a loser that I couldn't tell when I'd won." I blew every last dollar and was reduced to ringing my parents and asking them to pay for a ticket back to London.

I was devastated and it showed. When my parents met me at Heathrow, they hardly recognised me. My skin was bad, my eyes were sunken, and my frame was nearly emaciated. I looked exactly like the drug addict I was. When my mother saw me, she burst into tears... but they still had no idea. Naive as she was, mum thought my condition was down to a lack of nutrition and that I just needed a few home-cooked meals and some time to rest.

6

FROM HOLLYWOOD TO OAKWOOD

After approximately a year and a half, I'd now swapped Hollywood, California for Oakwood, Enfield — a suburb of a suburb where my parents were now living. I had no job and no future, although it turned out that the acting classes I'd taken weren't a total waste of my time.

When I tried withdrawing from crack and alcohol, I failed. With my body starting to convulse as the alcohol left my system, and lacking the will power to see it through, I started drinking again... and soon I started smoking cannabis once again as well. Before long I'd managed to track down a crack dealer, a Jamaican by the name of Yogi who operated out of Earls Court.

The first time I saw him I'd been drinking in a pub called the Prince of Tec — he might as well have had the word "dealer" tattooed on his forehead. Although he looked quite menacing, after what I'd been through in LA this was nothing new to me. Without a second thought I approached him and asked for a "bone," a little rock of crack that looks a lot like a sugar lump. Even though it was a *lot* more expensive than in Los Angeles, £100 later I had *five* bones and a pipe.

The upside of crack is that it gives you an intense, euphoric high. Immediately after smoking it you experience a rush, temporarily heightened senses, and a feeling that you've never been as alive as you are at that precise moment in time. The downside is that it turns you into both a physical wreck… and a *fucking idiot*.

When you smoke it, the high lasts for only five to ten minutes and even if you inject, it seldom endures for more than half an hour. Your pupils look like rabbit droppings, your appetite vanishes, your heart starts beating like the "fucked clock" from the film *Withnail & I*… and almost immediately you need another hit. Worse yet, if it isn't immediately available you can become paranoid, depressed, and a risk to both yourself and others. I smoked the five bones that I'd just bought, one after the other, then spent the night sleeping rough in Earls Court, surrounded by crack and heroin addicts, before stumbling home on the tube the following morning.

———————

WITH MY LIFE GOING nowhere, my mother asked my uncles, her brothers, if they would give me an opportunity to work in the family firm, the 'TRS Cash and Carry' and wholesale business.

They agreed, reluctantly I feel, although they were too polite to tell her about any reservations that they might have had about trusting me with their business.

TRS had become a successful brand, especially in the Asian retail market, and they're still thriving today as trs.co.uk. Working for the business made my mother proud and I was eventually put in charge of the ethnic foods section. However, as my drug use was beginning to have serious side effects — I started to suffer from depression as well as collapsing a few times due to drug and alcohol-induced exhaustion — I only lasted about a year and a half. Working for the family business had taken its toll on me and in realizing this, I duly resigned.

Eventually, I made the decision to stop drinking alcohol, although I continued to smoke cannabis daily and had a crack binge once a week. Needless to say, to fund these habits I needed a new job. Staying in the retail business, I switched from the safe, but dull, food sector to the expanding (and lucrative) narcotics division.

For one, I'd started hanging out with Big Black again. Since I'd last seen him he'd moved up in the world... specifically, the underworld... and was now in the habit of carrying a Beretta 9mm pistol, which he'd use to help part £5,000 worth of weed from a dealer down in Brighton.

He'd acquired the weed thanks to an elaborate set up involving his childhood friend, Trevor, who was supposed to be doing a 25-year stretch but had been released on appeal after just ten months. This happened because the authorities couldn't explain how he'd moved the victim from the scene of the crime to a deserted woodland, so due to this lack of evidence his conviction was now downgraded to being a simple "altercation."

Trevor had met this dealer in a park in Brighton, pretending that he had money to purchase 10kg of Thai weed. During the meeting Big Black turned up and beat the shit out of both Trevor and the dealer. Big Black was a professional, knowing exactly the amount of violence needed to administer a convincing, but non-lethal assault. Using a knuckle-duster, he knocked them both out and then stole the weed. When he finally came to, Trevor was battered enough to be able to play the victim. Furiously, he went away claiming that he'd been set up and threatened all sorts of vengeance on the people who'd wronged him, when in reality it was him all the time. With the weed in their possession, Big Black and Trevor now split it between themselves and the rest was history.

I never really got on with Trevor... this may have been due to a bit of jealousy on both of our parts, as I guess I felt that I was Big Black's best friend and Trevor felt the same. So still feeling this way, when Big Black asked me to sell his share of the weed for him, I agreed. It wasn't an offer that I couldn't refuse. Although I did feel some pressure from him for this "favor," I still could have backed out if I'd wanted to.

Instead, I found the idea of playing a gangster to be quite seductive. I had a contact in Walthamstow, quite literally just around the corner from TRS in Leyton, who worked in a warehouse there. Thus began my first, as well as one of my most lucrative, roles as an actor. To be convincing in this part I had to act as if I wasn't shitting myself whilst I accompanied Big Black to "Lock Stock" territory in an East London drug den — all the while holding enough hash to get me five years in the kind of place that would make Pierrepoint look like Champney's Health Spa.

Because I had absolute faith in Big Black, the consequences of failure hadn't even entered my head and because of this I was able to pull it off.

As we entered the house all the lights were off. In place of electric lights, we were escorted upstairs by a black guy holding a torch (flashlight). Eventually we made our way into this room where there must've been about 20 black guys, all looking moody with their hoods up, bouncing to an NWA tune, making me feel like I was back in South Central LA.

Now having their attention, Big Black subtly pulled the front of his jacket back slightly to show them that he had a gun stashed in his trousers. Even though it was demonstrative rather than threatening, it was still a move that could have seriously backfired. Instead, when I looked around the room I could see one of the guests was bricking himself... noticing this made my confidence surge.

He handed over a sample for the buyer to try and the buyer liked it. With this, Big Black handed over the weed and they handed over the cash, offering us four grand for the lot. In the interests of making a quick sale and getting the fuck out of there, we accepted. Before concluding the transaction, I sat there counting the money while trying my best to look unflustered — little did they know that my heart was racing at somewhere close to 180 bpm (or more) and my bowels were doing somersaults.

When we finally walked out of there with the money, I realised that this was the role that I'd dreamed of, and trained for, all my life. Now that I'd pulled it off, I realised how much this lifestyle actually *turned me on.*

Perhaps the stress was getting to me, because my cannabis habit evolved and I began smoking an eighth of skunk a day. (It was, and still is, the heaviest marijuana out there, mixed with loads of THC and God knows what else.)

Consuming an eighth of skunk every week meant that I needed a constant supply of funds. For a while I raised the money by doing a bit of dealing, but even then I was together enough to realise that this probably wasn't a good idea. So instead of dealing, I did a bit of what I'll call 'debt collecting' with Big Black.

Then I fell in love.

7

LOVE AND MARRIAGE

I met my wife, Mehz, while travelling in India and within a year we were married. Given that I was a product of the English Public Schooling system it was no surprise that I didn't have an extensive knowledge of the opposite sex. Even though by this time I'd known a few women, I had yet to experience a deeper level of attraction with any one of them. However, in the moment when I first met Mehz, the attraction was instantaneous... I can honestly say that it was love at first sight.

Our wedding was a wonderful experience, a traditional Indian pageant that lasted for two whole weeks. For one part of the ceremony I was dressed like a prince on horseback in Mumbai, with six women in front of me with lanterns on their heads and a live band playing. It was all part of the ritual. My family walked to the bride's home where I symbolically asked her father if I could marry her.

For a brief period of time it felt like we were living in a fairytale, but at one of the many functions I found myself suddenly jolted back into reality. All around me were members of both our families who were drinking and, swept away by the occasion, I joined them. Even though I'd had my stomach pumped — and even though I'd been drinking since the age of 11 — I still didn't realise at the time that I was an addict. In hindsight it should have been obvious, but I had no idea that just *one* drink would set me off again.

The long-term consequences were brought home once we'd came back to the UK, where Mehz was now experiencing a culture shock, and my condition wasn't helping. I was a bum. I resumed my skunk habit with a vengeance, using my as yet undiscovered acting talents to convince her that my soporific lifestyle was entirely normal. Everyday life in India was hectic, set against a backdrop of almost permanent chaos, and by comparison, suburban London was tranquil. Somehow I managed to convince her that my inertia was nothing unusual.

Even so, I think it's possible that she was regretting getting married... not because of me but because of the move. While things got progressively worse, she still had no idea that I was an addict — and I was still in total denial.

Within a year we had our first child — a daughter — so I guess that's what kept her busy because I was too wired at the time to notice. It didn't help that our traditional roles were reversed... she was the one who was working and I was not. My daughter was about one when, courtesy of my father (who paid all of the fees), we put her in a private nursery. While I was obviously very grateful for his generosity, I was actually even more grateful that I could actually continue to do what I wanted to do — spend my days smoking weed and chilling out.

Still I hadn't quite given up on my dream of becoming an actor. In 1999 I got a call from one of the Twins' sisters-in-law, a casting director who asked me to audition for a film that was being made in London called, *It Was An Accident*. While I 'ummed' and 'ahhed' for a bit, I eventually went in to read for the main bad guy part... that of an Asian gangster.

As a result of this first audition, I was shortlisted and finally got down to the final two, but the other guy got the part. Why? The producer felt that he had the specific look that this part needed.

However, that wasn't the end because they gave me a small part that I knew was a great opportunity. While some of the cast would go on to great things, others, like James Bolam, had already done them. Chiwetel Ejiofor was the star, playing the part of an ex-con who was trying to go straight. Yet, merely by walking into the wrong bank at the wrong time, he gets dragged back into a life of crime. The love interest was a policeman's daughter played by Thandie Newton. Paul Chowdry had a cameo, and I was in a scene with Max Beesley, who happened to be a fantastic actor.

I really enjoyed the experience, especially having a car pick me up from my home and being in my own trailer on the set. This alone made me feel like a star... and being the method actor that I am, I stunk the place out smoking copious amounts of weed in my trailer. Finally when it was time for me to begin filming my part, upon opening the trailer door a massive amount of smoke poured out onto the set — I guess I looked the part. Whether I needed to be stoned while I had the shit beaten out of me I'm not sure, but at least it didn't hurt as much. While it was a great film, it was a flop at the cinema, probably because they picked the other guy instead of me! (Wink!) Altogether I was in four scenes, even though one of them ended up on the cutting room floor. So now, at the age of 24 I could say that I'd achieved one of my greatest lifetime ambitions, and I still have an IMDB page to this day.

When that was over I carried on acting like a bum, the only difference being that I wasn't getting paid for it any more. However, I got away with being a bum, without too much pressure from my family, because I could legitimately claim that I was student, which, to the untrained eye, is basically the same thing. I studied for a diploma in Psychodynamic Therapy, which I completed and passed, and also worked in a domestic violence centre where I was voluntarily counselling women.

Yet, this is where my ongoing drug problem was, once again, my downfall. While women would come to me with their problems, I was too high to care — it all went in one ear and out the other. Oddly enough, it turns out that the correct response to, "My husband's been beating me," is not silence accompanied by comatosed indifference. I tried to study Systemic Therapy too, but after six months I lost interest.

Then I got the chance to run a petrol station, although even in this situation I had to cheat. It turns out that all of the candidates had to go through a series of tests to earn a franchise and although I passed the English set with flying colours, maths was another matter. However, this is one occasion when I put my resourceful nature to good use. There was a Sri Lankan guy sitting the same exam and since I knew that Sri Lankans were supposed to be good at maths, I made sure that I sat next to him, copied his answers, and got 100 percent. I knew I'd performed well in the interview and with the experience I had, and the various roles that I'd performed, I was accepted. Luckily for me, there wasn't a practical component in this exam.

I'd worked at B&Q for a year before I got married and finally landed a cushy job as a manager. Unfortunately I was so stoned one day that while cutting a box with a Stanley knife, I sliced open my entire hand, only just missing a main artery. Wrapping it up, they took me to the hospital for treatment, but when the nurse removed the dressing she screamed as a jet of blood spurted out that nearly hit the ceiling. This "accident" left me with a massive scar… a reminder of what a life like the one I'd chosen for myself could do.

Here my life took an unexpected change of direction. I was supposed to be running a petrol station for Shell in Muswell Hill, but at the last minute they asked if I could take on a station in Maidstone in Kent instead. I had been having a few problems at home with my wife and my parents and, for the sake of everyone's sanity, this offer felt like a chance to get away. The other reason for doing this was to get away from London, the lifestyle, and the friends   those like Goldie, Big Black, and my Bangladeshi drug dealer. At least that was the plan.

For those of you who haven't yet had the pleasure, Kent is quite white and in some ways living there reminded me of my time in boarding school. Back in the year 2000 it was an area with very few non-whites. I can't remember seeing any Asian faces when I arrived, especially not in Leybourne, the village outside West Malling where we first lived.

Even when we relocated to be closer to the thriving cultural metropolis that is Maidstone town centre, there still weren't many Asians or Afro-caribbeans. This was a bit of a shock, as apart from the six years I'd spent in Frensham, I'd lived my entire life in London, a city of true cultural diversity. However, coming to Kent gave me the same feelings that I'd had at school. The lack of cultural diversity that I'd previously experienced was reflected through the lack of the kind of shops and restaurants that we'd become accustomed to in North London.

To start off with, we'd rented a property in Leybourne, but I found it was a bit of a distance to travel to the garage on Blue Bell Hill, so we moved into a nice chalet bungalow in Maidstone itself, just round the corner from *Her Majesty's Hotel*, which has in its time, offered hospitality to criminals the likes of both Reggie Kray and Jonathan King. We've been there ever since. Every single day when I pass the prison and its giant stone wall, I often remind myself how lucky I was to remain outside its walls.

By 2003 my son was born, my daughter was in primary school, and I was trying to run a petrol station. This wasn't as easy as it might have been because I was still smoking copious amounts of skunk. Almost immediately, my plan to leave London had backfired as I'd found a local dealer and started my own business dealing on the side. I must admit that I didn't do this to make money, but simply as a means of funding my own habit — I'd break up an ounce and sell it on. As I was still drinking heavily, I wasn't really paying much attention to what was going on with the business at the petrol station.

The garage was a foot off the A229, right by the junction for the M20. The whole area was a huge transport hub, which could have potentially been a goldmine, but we only made 1p per litre on the petrol and all of that basically went to pay staff wages. It was also a 24-hour operation, and in hindsight I probably could have done more hours myself and made a bit more money that way. While I did make *some* money on the food and confectionery, we ended up taking a loss because I wanted to help someone out.

I had a couple of Asian employees who'd been really desperate for work. They showed me their National Insurance numbers and their details looked kosher, so as I wanted to help them out, I took them on. Little did I know at the time that one of them was running a childishly simple, but very effective scam.

When a customer wanted to pay for an item in cash, he'd press the PLU button rather than actually scan the item. As it made a beep and the price came up on the screen, the customer wouldn't have noticed that anything was wrong. However, what the customer didn't realize was that the transaction wasn't going into the system. This particular employee would do this with any high-value items, like cigarettes, and put that money in his pocket.

He'd already scammed me out of £6000 when another member of staff, Harry, blew the whistle. He'd been feeling guilty for not speaking out earlier, and also told me that, while the guy was in the country he'd also been using a fake national insurance number. That got me a bit worried and I should have called the police.

Instead, I put a call in to Big Black, who came down from London. I asked the employee to come into the office and sat him down. Big Black then put his Beretta in the guys mouth, smacked him with the butt a couple of times under the chin, and then put his knuckle-dusters on and smacked him in the ribs several times. This all happened whilst I was there, witnessing it all. Needless to say, I was in shock.

It was only after this that we went to the police. Although he was deported, I never got my six grand back. When I reflect back on this instance, I can easily say that I was frightened. It wasn't the right thing to do then, and it's not what I'm about now. I also feel quite sad that it happened because of me... but that's where my drug and alcohol abuse had taken me.

The more immediate result was that I lost the franchise. Having lost all that money, Shell asked me to leave, so my next venture was to open up a car wash in Maidstone, located on a side street off Upper Stone Street. I named it Low-Dosh Car Wash. At first we didn't get a lot of through traffic, so I had signs made that I placed on the side of the road directing traffic right to our entrance. Thankfully, it worked! For a labor force, I recruited quite a lot of Eastern Europeans, Poles, and Albanians — those who traditionally performed that kind of work. I also went around getting contracts with car companies in the area, offering them better rates than they were currently getting. *This* business did well.

While it might sound mundane, the car wash industry led me into some even crazier experiences that, unbeknownst to me, were lying in wait not very far ahead.

8

CAR WARS

Call it delusional, but there was a time when I imagined that the Low Dosh Car Wash might become Maidstone's equivalent of the Bada Bing Club, or Satriale's Pork Store. However, instead it evolved into something more like the A1 Car Wash from *Breaking Bad*, albeit on a drastically reduced scale.

To anyone who passed it, it wouldn't have looked like anything other than a mundane, back street car cleaning operation. But as far as I was concerned, it was the foundation stone for my new business empire.

The idea came to me when I was getting my own car cleaned. At the time I was driving a massive Jeep Grand Cherokee, with huge bass speakers in the back that would pump out gangsta rap like 2Pac, Biggie Smalls, and Snoop Dogg at a decibel level that the entire world could hear, whether it wanted to or not.

I used to go to a car wash in Strood, and when I saw how busy it was I thought to myself, "I'd fancy a piece of this." Just like a *maitre d'* in a hotel or restaurant, there was this African guy who was the front man there, and it wasn't long before we started talking about the business. This encounter planted the idea in my head, and as soon as it took root there was nothing that was going to dissuade me from starting my own car wash. I also knew who I wanted to run it… my new African friend who was so dedicated that I'd decided to head hunt him.

The first problem we had to overcome was our location. The A229 is one of the busiest, most congested roads in the South of England, outside London, and the passing cars can pick up a layer of filth in a matter of seconds, so without a doubt there was plenty of demand. Our "problem" was that we were a few metres away on Salem Street where there was *almost no passing traffic.*

I temporarily solved this by buying a giant neon sign that I placed on the main road, but even then the footfall was intermittent and it took me a while to work out just why this was the case.

On one occasion I went to the main road and saw that the sign had been moved and flattened. As it had a hard, water-filled base, there was no way that it could have been blown that far by accident. However, I thought that this might just have been due to either some casual vandalism or perhaps a student prank.

Putting it back in place, I went back to the car wash and didn't think a lot more about it until one time when I happened to be driving up Upper Stone Street and suddenly saw two guys moving it. I followed them until I saw them walk into another car wash up the road, at which point I realised what was going on.

The rival car wash was run by members of the local Albanian community who had earned a certain reputation. Albania was, and still is, one of the most deprived countries in Europe and so people who'd emerged from that chaos carried a certain cachet about themselves. If there was one thing that everyone knew it was that you did *not fuck with the Albanians.*

I, on the other hand, didn't have many options. While I might have been living in an almost permanent, drug-induced haze, I was still astute enough to know that calling the police was neither a smart idea nor an option. I think that they believed that I was a bigger villain than I actually was, so needless to say they weren't going to be interested in helping me. However, for my part I thought I was getting away with something, and doing anything that would unnecessarily draw attention to myself didn't seem like it would be a great idea.

So instead, I made alternative arrangements and rang a couple of people whom I knew locally, and within an hour they'd assembled a multi-national coalition of mixed-race hardcases, hard-hitting Eastern Europeans, and ex-cons, of whom there were plenty to call on given that Maidstone is home to one of Her Majesty's most popular residential franchises.

At that time, our weapon of choice was the baseball bat, which could be purchased from all good sports shops as well as the bigger, less reputable chains, despite the fact that, in terms of participation, baseball ranks lower than either badminton or tiddlywinks. The good news was that there were no restrictions on ownership.

"Hey Vladimir, nice to see you again."

"How can I help?"

"Twenty-four baseball bats, please."

"Oh, are you starting a team?"

"No. I practice in Mote Park with friends."

In a move that was only meant to give them a warning, we destroyed the rival car wash. While I'm not proud of it now, that was the kind of life that I was in… you mess with *my* business, I mess with *yours*. I didn't like doing it, but I felt that I had to — and to some extent it paid off.

Having violated the unwritten law about not fucking with Albanians, I was pretty sure that there'd be some kind of comeback, so I rang Big Black, who came down from London... one of my better ideas.

The next day two of the Albanian bosses came into my carwash, and Big Black's presence stopped things from escalating. If he hadn't been there it might well have gone another way, but when I explained why we'd done what we'd done, they agreed that they wouldn't move the sign again and we both called a truce. In fact, we even went on to do some other business together, which I'll not go into here.

However, there still was a problem... even after we'd resolved this matter, the car wash *still* wasn't making the kind of money that I'd anticipated. In fact, for a while it wasn't making any money at all.

The workforce was mainly Polish and Albanian, and for a while I was paying them out of my own pocket, until one of the Polish guys asked me if I could get him some speed. I told him that I'd ask around... and as one of my contacts had recently moved into the speed business, we did a deal. It was pure, and incredibly cheap, and as a result some of the workers weren't actually working for cash at all. I paid them in speed, one of the fringe benefits being that the cars were getting cleaned very thoroughly and unbelievably quickly because so many of the workers were amped up on speed.

After a while we tried branching out because there was a gap in the market for the refurbishment of alloy wheels. The nearest place that did anything like that was in Gillingham (about 15 km, or 10 miles, away) and they were charging double what I was at over £100 per wheel. I had a fantastic Slovakian colleague, called George, who was so good at what he did that I thought we could do the whole car for around the same price. However, we *still* weren't making the money that I'd imagined we could.

Further diversification was needed, so I moved back into the cannabis sector, with a sideline dealing cocaine, storing it all in the office above the ceiling panels in the waiting room. Altogether there were two kilos of skunk up there, along with a few ounces of coke. The smell was so strong that I might as well have put up an LCD display system with an arrow pointing to the stash with the words "Get Your Drugs Here" scrolling across the front.

The irony in all of this was that some of our *best customers* belonged to Her Majesty's police force. The car wash was handily positioned between the town centre and their HQ on Sutton Road, which happened to be nestled between some of the town's most exclusive residential areas, like Shepway, Mangravet, and Park Wood.

Skunk is not a great scent for a car wash; no air freshener in the world can mask it. Yet, for whatever reason, the clientele were either too polite to mention it, or they didn't care. Possibly both. Whenever anyone asked I blamed it on the customers. *"Yeah, you know, some of the people we get in here, you wouldn't believe it. But what can you do?"*

They had no idea as to the size of the stash that was directly above their heads.

This worked for a while, but it didn't really make me any money as it was mainly in place to fund my own habit. While at this time I wasn't touching cocaine, cannabis, skunk, and alcohol were my drugs of choice… and I was doing a lot of all of them, smoking up to two ounces of cannabis a week, something that I'd been doing for 15 years.

Oh, I was still binging on alcohol, having 30 units (roughly 750 ml, aka a 'fifth') a week of vodka, gin, whisky, *and* sambuca. Everyone else in the car wash was drinking too, especially the ones who were doing speed. Big Black was also coming in on a daily basis, mainly to make sure that nothing went wrong with drug sales, but also for general security. We paid him in weed, free drinks, and my wife's incredibly delicious home cooking.

The reason that the car wash didn't become something like Satriale's was because I didn't have a Soprano work ethic. I was happy to do the bit where they'd sit around all day, but I left the dirty work to others. All I did was sit in my jeep with our babysitter and smoke weed. Looking back, I wonder if someone who was that stoned was real au pair material. Yet, at the time I was too stoned to know, or care.

I had no idea what was going on in the outside world... and you can only get away with that for so long.

9
—————

YOU LOOK LIKE A DRUG ADDICT

uddenly conscious of their mortality when they hit their thirties, some people slow down. However, at the same time (and for the same reason), others go in the opposite direction, desperate to cram in as much as they can, while they can. You don't need to be a detective to work out which path I chose.

My fourth decade was a time of overpowering grief, which I coped with through reckless hedonism. In fact it was due to my drug-addled senses that — even though I nearly lost my senses (both physically as well as metaphorically) — I thought I could live like a god. However, in spite of such recklessness, my business career finally took off, and as a result I began making tens of thousands of pounds per month, only to blow it all. While over the previous three decades I'd fractured numerous laws and gotten away with it, after becoming the victim of an assault that nearly blinded me (and forcing a team of medical experts to rebuild my face) I would finally get arrested.

Here I was at the age of 30 with a beautiful wife, a daughter in primary school, and a newly born son. As far as money was concerned, the car wash, now being run by our babysitter, was still a going concern. In all honesty, when she agreed to look after our children she probably never thought that she'd end up running a business.

From the outside it must have looked as though I had everything going for me. Yet fate was about to deal a savagely cruel hand when my mother was diagnosed with abdominal cancer. At almost exactly the same time a cholesteatomatic tumour was detected on the back of my ear. While it was benign, it was still growing up towards my brain, and had it gone undetected it could have caused serious complications, including brain damage.

I needed mastoid surgery and luckily we had private medical insurance so it was taken care of quickly enough. However, the doctor, a Spaniard by the name of Oyarzabal, came into my room to tell me that in 17 years of surgery this was the biggest growth that he'd ever removed. That was the good news... the bad news was that it left me 80 percent deaf in my left ear. To this day I continue to have regular ENT outings, during which a tube will be stuck in my ear, they'll flush it out, and check for any complications.

Around about the time that my son had his first birthday, my mum passed away. Her illness and death affected me big time because we were very, very close. However, instead of making me realise just how precious life is, I dealt with it by increasing my drug intake. Some of her very last words to me were, and I quote, "you look like a drug addict."

This was maybe two to three days before she passed, and for her to say it then was very shocking for me to hear. It was also weird for the fact that she'd never mentioned anything about either my drink habit, the reek of skunk that she must have smelt every time I walked past her, or the red eyes that I tried to cover up with the eye drops that I always had with me.

Soon afterwards the car wash dissolved as it had stopped making money. What this meant is that I couldn't get the speed that I needed to pay the eastern Europeans. The only one who stayed with me was Slovakian George, who I'd subsequently hired as my driver. While I was still going out a lot, the ear operation had affected my balance, so for a while I couldn't drive on motorways. Instead of giving him cash, I paid him by getting him into the top clubs in London like Distrkt, Alto, and Crystal, where I had VIP memberships. These were places where they'd charge you £2000 just to get in, although it was dressed up as a "minimum spend." In that context, the £500 per person VIP membership cost for 12 months didn't actually seem that bad, especially as it allowed me to bring in two guests... and guests were one thing I was never short of.

It wasn't long before cocaine came into my life in a big way. One of the side effects of this happening was that my circle of friends was beginning to evolve and expand. First I fell in with a Mauritian guy, called Ahmet, whom I'd been impressed by ever since he'd brought his Porsche to my garage, then later the car wash.

Then there was Mark, the window cleaner — a man who'd introduced me to a life-changing property deal. We bought a beautiful sub penthouse in Bromley South that, at the time, was worth about £350k. It was next door to a property owned by Chelsea FC that had been used to provide temporary accommodation for new signings. At that time the English footballer (soccer player for you Americans) Shaun Wright-Phillips was living there.

Along with a Greek guy, yet another George, the four of us bought the property together. Under the terms of the deal we got £10-15k cash back in our hands. For me, this was a 'eureka' moment! However, as quickly as Greek George was teaching me how to *make* money, Ahmet and Slovakian George were helping me *spend* it. Two or three times a week we'd meet up in the car park of a pub in Maidstone, called Hanrahans, where we'd do some coke, then drive to London where we'd spend the money I'd been making.

Needless to say, after my Mum passed away this lifestyle escalated. I'm not using it as an excuse, just as an explanation for some of the madness that followed.

Using this cashback scheme that I'd learned from Greek George, I bought another three properties and suddenly had more money than I'd ever seen in my life... with no idea what to do with it. It was then that something took me over.

I don't know if I was buying them because I wanted to get on the property ladder, or because I wanted the cash, but instead of saving it, I started reliving the gangsta fantasy — hiring Bentleys and driving to clubs with a stash full of drugs that I knew the valet wouldn't touch because he *knew* that I was with Big Black.

These were the kind of places where footballers, film stars, and musicians used to hang out. We'd regularly see people like Rio Ferdinand, Amir Khan, Leona Lewis, and Rihanna. I once happened to have a dance with Jessie J even though, at the time, she had a broken leg. We'd get a private table and spend ridiculous amounts of money on Dom Perignon and Cristel champagne. In slang terms it was called flossing — flaunting your lifestyle on things that made you look like you're wealthy.

I became friendly with the manager, a guy called Fraser, who'd probably taken a shine to me because I was giving him so much of my newly-found fortune.

While I could have spent this time bonding with my young children, instead I was spending money that wasn't mine — and gambling with things that I didn't have — while I bonded with Slovakian George, with whom I became particularly close at this time. Whilst this was partly because he was driving me everywhere, it was mainly due to our shared love of coke.

The buzz it produced was unlike anything I'd experienced… either before, or since. When I was on it I didn't care about anything or anyone else. Over time it started to take control of my life. A typical night would involve Ahmet and I having a couple of grammes, after which he'd sensibly go home. For the next round I'd pick up Slovakian George and get him to drive my Mercedes S-class to Edmonton, near where I used to live in North London. From there we'd pick up the complimentary Bentley that Big Black's contacts had arranged for us for the evening.

We'd floss the whole night, finally getting back at around 6 the next morning. (This all sounds great until you realise that my kids basically didn't have a father and I was ignoring my wife.) So this was the cycle of my life… at night I'd be out flossing, and when the coke finally wore off I'd be home sleeping it off.

If my Dad, who at this time was now in his late seventies, had noticed my behaviour, he didn't say anything. He was still grieving and maybe I was too, but nonetheless, I wasn't taking any responsibility for anything that was in front of me. From there things would only get worse.

While working for Greek George I met a Turkish guy who'd just gotten out of jail for something involving firearms. For some odd reason, more than likely all of the drugs that fogged my judgment, he sounded like an ideal business partner. It wasn't long before we decided to set up our own property company, Buxton Marks, with an office in Canary Wharf. We came up with the name by taking the Bux from my surname and the surname of our third, female partner, Marks. While it sounded (and on a business card, looked) professional, I think it rankled the Turkish partner whose name wasn't used.

No matter what, this probably something that he didn't care to voice because he was incredibly hungry for success — which more than likely came from the fact that he'd just been released. I found both these attributes, if that's the right word, of his to be quite 'attractive' overall.

And for a while it all seemed to work. We operated in a 'legally grey' area that was *slightly* bent without being *so* bent that anyone actually would crack down on it. It was like being on a motorway with a speed limit of 65 mph when everyone else was doing 85 mph… so we did it too.

We built up relationships with anyone who was building new properties. They had a system to encourage people to buy property whereby they'd not only pay your deposit, but they'd also give you cash back. It was the same principle as getting an extra £20 in notes after doing your weekly food shop. You weren't getting free money, but it *felt* like you were.

So far, so legal. However, this was where the chicanery came in.

A surveyor would value a property worth £100k at £110k. We would then get a mortgage company, one I won't name, to give us a loan worth 90 percent of the value of the property and we could pay the balance using the cash back. While it seemed too good to be true, the numbers all checked out so armed with this information we decided to buy an entire block. Soon we started working with consortia from South Africa and Sri Lanka who'd buy entire complexes, knowing that we'd both get £10,000 for every single property that it contained.

Yet even when things were good there was still a human cost.

I had a falling out with the twins because they thought I was ripping them off… something that still hurts me to this day. While I got them into the property scheme and made them some money, when one of them saw that the same property was on sale for less elsewhere, he thought that I was conning them. The truth was that it was *all* a con — just one that happened to be legal — and one that benefited us all.

Their blindspot in this situation was that they couldn't see that they were as much a part of it as I was. Even now when I think about the loss of what had once been a deep, binding friendship, I still feel gutted.

At one point I was earning £60,000 a month. The only problem was that I was spending £80,000 on drink, drugs, cars, and gambling. I was delusional and incredibly irresponsible. Even though I did get stopped a couple of times while driving drunk, high, or both, all of this activity seemed completely normal.

Once, after picking up my brother-in-law from the airport, we went to Crystal, where I drank an entire bottle of Belvedere Vodka, followed by an eighth of cocaine. As we were driving back through the East End I noticed a police car behind me, so I got paranoid and tried to lose it.

All of a sudden it became a cop chase, one in which I was diving in and out of side streets until we got stopped on Vallance Road, not far from where I'd grown up — and bang in the middle of a street full of working girls and crack dealers.

In a matter of minutes I was arrested and taken to Bethnal Green police station, whilst my brother-in-law remained in the car for about six hours surrounded by pimps and prostitutes. Even though I was well over the limit and in the cell for a few hours, for some bizarre reason the cops finally decided let me off on a caution. So somewhere around seven the next morning I walked back to my car. The only explanation I can think of for doing what they did is that they must have connected me with Big Black and let me off because they were hoping to get me on something bigger. However, as I wasn't directly involved with Big Black's more interesting work, that was never going to happen.

Drunk driving with my brother-in-law was one thing. Drug driving with my daughter was on another level entirely.

My behavioural nadir came when I needed to buy some coke while I was supposed to be looking after my little girl. On the one hand I didn't want to expose her to the kind of business I was doing. However, on the other hand, I *needed* the coke.

Faced with this dilemma, I devised a compromise. The car I was driving at the time had a built in entertainment system with a big screen TV and DVD player in the back. I drove to one of my properties where I left her watching a film while I went upstairs to not only do the deal, but tried a couple of lines in the bargain. Two hours later I *finally* came back down to the car and drove the two of us home. In spite of the time that I'd been away, she was none the wiser because she'd been occupied by the film, completely unaware that my behaviour as a parent might be considered abnormal.

My condition was basically IGS — Imaginary Gangsta Syndrome. I wore shades all the time, even in nightclubs; I wore sharp suits; and having a mate like Big Black, along with a driver like Slovakian George, made me think that I was a *big* man. Wads of cash would disappear in three or four hours and I'd be forced to make another move to get even more cash from another unknowing source.

In many ways I thought I was John Gotti, but the flipside of living in this manner was the risk of violence. While I didn't have nearly as many enemies — and certainly not the type who'd order a calculated hit — nothing can completely inoculate you from the danger that someone, somewhere, will take exception to you in the least likely of times and places.

Maidstone's Chicago Rock Cafe had a reputation for being a last chance saloon for desperate menopausal women who were looking for a Saturday night pull. While it was the sort of place where Gotti wouldn't have been seen dead, we went there for a drink whilst I was waiting for my cocaine dealer to deliver. Once this had taken place, we'd make our way back to London.

While I was looking in the vague direction of six travellers, I noticed that Big Black was talking to a woman. One of the six whom I just happened to glance at thought that this was an act of provocation, and with that, he approached me as he fired off the classic line, "What are *you* looking at?"

"I'm not looking at nothing," I replied.

Maybe he was offended by the double negative, but for whatever reason, this answer didn't satisfy him. He pushed me, so I pushed him back. Big Black was still deep in conversation and didn't see what was happening until it was too late. Without warning, this 'traveller' picked up a pint glass and rammed it into my face with such violence that I didn't know what had hit me.

I retaliated by giving him a headbutt, then somehow managed to tap Big Black on the arm. When he turned round I saw a look of undiluted horror on his face. Given the kind of things that he must have seen in his life, this was not the least bit reassuring.

"Who did that to you?" he spat.

"Them," I replied, waving in the direction of the five men who were about to do me.

Putting his knuckle dusters on, one after the other, he basically knocked all five of them out. While this had solved one problem, since Big Black was already wanted by the Police, it created another. We were both arrested, although in my case the punishment was going to have to wait as my face was peeling off.

They immediately transferred me to the specialist hospital in East Grinstead the was famous for its work on fire victims and war veterans. In the surgery that followed, they reconstructed a quarter of my face, and as a result now there are five titanium plates where I used to have a cheek bone. The injury ended up being so close to my eye that I was lucky that I didn't lose it.

Even today, all of these years later, the pain sometimes comes back to remind me of that night.

When the police took me home, and my wife initially saw the state of my face, she nearly fainted. However, to their credit, they told her the truth — that I'd been attacked by six people. While the charges against me were dropped, Big Black had been put in a cell. I bailed him out, but he was later fined for GBH (grievous bodily harm, otherwise known as assault). Whilst my attackers were given a £250 fine and community service, to crown it all the story appeared, along with *my picture and home address*, in the Kent Messenger, neatly advertising my whereabouts to my attackers just in case they fancied getting any retribution.

The fallout of this incident was significant. By the time I was fully discharged, I'd lost my job and most all of the money that I'd made was gone. Despite all of this, I was still faithful and loyal to my addictions.

To their credit, the job that the surgeons at East Grinstead did on my face late that evening was nothing short of a miracle. To this day you'd never know that someone had rammed a pint glass into my cheek. Along with a slight scar on the top of my eye near the eyebrow, there's also a scar under my left eye where a bag would normally appear. On the other side there are five titanium plates.

Just after being discharged I still had quite a bit of money, which I invested in the gambling industry over the next few months. When these investments failed to pay off I realised that I needed another job. Since I'd also developed a new obsession with physical fitness, landing a job with TruGym in Maidstone should have been ideal as it would mean that I could earn money while I was training.

I did a lot of cardio work and was lifting weights, all of which were good. On the flipside, I was also still doing cocaine. As a keyholder, my job was to open the gym at 6 in the morning so that all of the early risers could get their sessions in before going to work. However, I would frequently still be high from the night before, so I'd often turn up with my eyes blazing red and coke all over my nose. While my skin is dark brown, the cocaine was making me look so white that I might as well have had the word 'addict' written on my forehead with a permanent marker. Even though it wasn't an attractive look, it did alert two of the customers to my suitability for yet another questionable business venture.

Soon I'd meet a couple of Chinese guys who were looking for people to run crystal meth for them. As I wasn't earning much at the gym (and as my coke and alcohol needs weren't going to fund themselves indefinitely) I decided that it was worth a go, even though I had no idea what crystal meth actually was. Neither, it seemed, did anyone else.

At the time there was no demand for it, so as an experiment of sorts I was given a patch in East London, around Stratford, Bromley-by-Bow, and Mile End to see if I could rid of it. Mind you, this was not a standard arrangement. I'd been given the product on credit and the returns were potentially enough to fund my habits *and* once again keep me in the lifestyle to which I wished to become accustomed. However, this arrangement had one real complication; I'd had to give them my passport and home address as security on the 'loan'.

As a result, a new routine developed in my life. By day, I was Saf Buxy, leisure industry professional, but by night I dealt crystal meth. Again this worked for a while, but it came at the expense of my family, whom, once again, I neglected. Needless to say, it didn't take long for me to realise that these two careers were incompatible.

Complaints about the quality of my gym work were beginning to pile up, something that wasn't very surprising given that I'd snort coke in the kitchen and then again off the bench press. As a keyholder I could open the premises whenever I liked, so I'd invite people over for parties in the middle of the night, either unaware that the security cameras were capturing absolutely everything on video, or simply delusional that anyone would actually care about these unsolicited soirees.

Then the inevitable happened and I was sacked. They called me into a meeting to tell me that they suspected me of selling drugs, although ironically enough they thought I was dealing in anabolic steroids — which were popular at the time with gym goers who wanted to build their muscles — but arguably far less serious than the substances I was actually offloading.

While they didn't even mention the parties, the upshot of it all was that now I was free to finally to concentrate on my second career as an ice broker.

One Friday I'd a party lined up at Club Crystal that a couple of celebrities, including the singers Estelle and Mary J Blige, were supposed to be attending. Slovakian George was planning to drive me in my S-class Mercedes to the usual pick-up point, where we'd swap it for a Bentley. The idea was to just go there and chill, by which I mean drink and snort coke. However, that morning I noticed that a light was on in the downstairs bathroom.

Making my way through the bathroom door, I found my Dad, collapsed on the floor with his eyes open. I was reluctant to move him in case he'd fallen, so I called an ambulance. He was taken to the hospital where they said that he may have suffered a heart attack, keeping him overnight for observation.

At that moment any *rational* human being would have put his life on hold, but since those faculties of mine were completely muted, instead I decided to go to the party, regardless of what had just happened to my dad. There I drank, snorted coke, and basked in the reflected glory of being in the same place as both Estelle and Rio Ferdinand.

Yet while I was there my phone rang, my wife's name flashing up on the screen. As I didn't want to answer it, I ignored the call, but it kept on ringing so insistently that I finally went outside and picked up. Mehz told me that I immediately had to go straight to the hospital, but wouldn't say why. This made me fear the worst and finally brought the gravity of the situation home to me. Hearing this, I told George that we had to go, but I was in no condition to drive so he drove the Bentley to the Merc, and then the Merc to Maidstone Hospital. Even *during* the journey, I was still doing copious amounts of cocaine, but this was to numb me to the realization of what I knew was soon to come.

When we arrived I was told that my dad had passed away — it remains one of the biggest regrets of my life that I wasn't there. The fact that I *still* went out hurts me more than anything else in the world. The two people who'd been with me for my entire life were now gone, and realizing this deeply broke me.

In accordance with Islamic tradition we buried him the next day, but during the service I was still coming down from the previous night's intake. I looked like a mess but I got away with it because everyone assumed it was purely grief. Trust me when I tell you that I wasn't faking that part as I was absolutely devastated. Just when you'd think that things couldn't get any worse, they only went downhill from there.

The next five years were probably the worst of my life as I broke the golden rule of any dealer… 'don't get high off your own supply'. Within a month of my father passing away I went to a block of flats opposite Bromley-by-Bow station, to meet a couple of Chinese guys with a view to doing a deal. They asked me what crystal meth was like, but because I'd never actually tried it, I couldn't tell them. One of them suggested that we rectify the situation and with those words he produced a pipe. I smoked it off some foil and suddenly I experienced one of the most incredible feelings that I've ever had —

a feeling of just not giving a shit, a feeling of immortality. I felt indestructible; powerful beyond words. For the next five years I was hooked and possessed by *the filthiest drug ever known to man*.

Mixing that with alcohol was already a recipe for disaster, but this was compounded when I started smoking what I should have been selling. I was quickly in so much debt that I gave my Mercedes S-class to my dealer. All that did was buy me some more time. The guys that I'd given my passport to had themselves passed it on to a Chinese mafioso organisation that specialised in people trafficking…the Snakeheads. These were the kind of men who would happily smuggle dissidents out of North Korea for a $50,000 dollar fee that would have to be paid back under conditions so gruelling that the dissidents would often end up wishing they'd stayed in the North.

The methods these people used meant that not only was my life in danger, but once again, I'd put my family at risk as well.

I had no idea what to do. The cashback scheme was worth another £15k, but I put £10k of that towards the debt and immediately put the rest down as a deposit for an M class Mercedes because I *still* wanted to have that image. Then another, life-changing opportunity arose, one that was, perhaps, the most surreal of the lot.

10

LASHINGS

The nearest bar to Low Dosh Car Wash was a place called Lashings, which became famous in the mid 1990s when they signed Richie Richardson, then the captain of the West Indies, to play for their cricket team. Its owner was a man by the name of David Folb who would bring his Aston Martin into Low Dosh where we'd always give it the best cleaning. He and I had always got on well. Even though I hadn't played since my days in school, I was a massive fan of cricket.

From the outside Lashings seemed to have evolved from a pub team into a slick, corporate entity, so I asked him for a job. It was when he agreed that I realised the team's exterior belied a more complex reality.

The job description was vague. Lashings was and still is an all-star cricket team, which travels around the UK playing exhibition matches against star-struck club cricketers in front of wealthy corporate audiences.

As part of my job description, I was supposed to book matches, attract sponsors, market events, liaise with the players, and ensure that everything went smoothly on match days. The last part alone was enough to keep someone occupied 24-7.

Yet this was further complicated by the fact that not only was someone else, a woman by the name of Sharon, already doing the job, but that David hadn't bothered to tell her that she was being replaced. I think the plan was for her to return to a management role in the office, but when I turned up for my first day and introduced myself, I was expecting her to talk me through the role. She thought that not only was I taking her job, but that she was supposed to train me how to do it! Once that misunderstanding had been cleared up, we thankfully got on quite well and I think she was quite glad she didn't have to travel to the matches any more, as she had absolutely no interest in cricket.

However, for someone like me, suddenly finding myself working with people like Saqlain Mushtaq, Gordon Greenidge, and other cricket stars, didn't help my already altered sense of reality. I'd gone from worshipping these men to becoming their colleague. I'd pick them up at airports, arrange their accommodations, sort out their expenses and wages, and act as their confidant. If they had a problem, my job was to fix it… and as I usually did, we got on well. I became good friends with Gordon and Saqqy and also got on well with Phillip DeFreitas, Devon Malcolm, John Emburey, Yasir Arafat, and the King himself, Sir Courtney Walsh.

By the same lot, I got on less well with Inzamam-ul-Haq, who was less able to pass incognito than some of his team mates. Asian cricketers are treated more like rock stars that sportsmen and some of them are better equipped to deal with it than others. Saqlain was, and still is, a deeply spiritual man who can cope with pretty much anything life throws at him. Inzy, on the other hand, was more easily flustered.

The pressure on him was less intense in England than it would have been in Pakistan, but on one occasion we were playing a tournament in Crawley and he had one his moments. The whole ethos of Lashings was that no one was allowed to refuse an autograph, but a sizeable number of Asian fans had turned up and they all wanted selfies with him and more.

After a while Inzy cracked and stormed off, refusing to play. My job was to convince him that he had to and even now I'm not sure if the experience was better or worse than handing over my S-Class Merc to the Chinese Mafia.

He sat in his car with his head in his hands, saying "Everyone wants a piece of me," and refusing to come out. It took every negotiating skill that I had to get him to reconsider, all time that I should have been spending to look after our sponsors and clients.

However, Inzy wasn't my only problem. As part of the club's ethos, Lashings staff were supposed to go "full kit" at events. This wasn't usually a problem for the auction girls and the road crew, but because I was the same age and build as some of the players, people started mistaking me for an international cricketer.

Even though most of the players saw the funny side of this assumption, it appeared to me that it irked Ed Giddins, who thought I was confusing myself with 'the talent'. In all fairness to him, perhaps I was. Fans were coming up to me and asking for autographs, which I had to sign *as refusal would have looked even worse.*

For the first time in my life I was living like the star that I'd always hoped I would become. Yet this didn't exactly reduce my appetite, or need, for narcotics. An hour of trying to persuade Inzy not to erupt would probably have made the Dalai Lama reach for the crack pipe and all the while David Folb was on the phone, every half an hour, asking me if something had been done.

The average job expectancy at Lashings was about three months, so I did well to last six. When the season ended I was burned out and I ended up working in the bar alongside Sharon's son Matt, who'd go on to win the X-factor in 2016.

It felt like a comedown and I dealt with it in the usual way. Working in a bar was the worst possible environment for someone with my issues, and as a result my addiction to alcohol (what I then called 'my drink habit') escalated.

At some point I thought a trip to the Hippodrome Casino would cure my worries. Just as I had in Vegas years earlier, I started well and at one point was £12k up. However, as I had also done in Vegas during that same time, I blew the lot. My way of dealing with that was to go to a crystal meth den in Chinatown… something that was another bad idea.

Two of my revellers were Snakeheads who recognised me and decided to ask what I was planning to do about the outstanding £7k that I owed them. They did this by bundling me into a corner and holding knives to various, vulnerable parts of my body. The message was clear: I had seven days to find the money or they were *going to fuck me up*.

11

CSI: MANGRAVET

How the hell was I supposed to get my hands on seven thousand pounds in seven days? I had no money left — my wages had gone, and I'd rinsed out both of my children's savings accounts. We had absolutely nothing and I was flat broke. However, it was in this desperate state that I hit upon a solution that, at the time, seemed like a good idea — I could sell my wife's jewellery. At Indian weddings the bride is given a lot of jewellery and Mehz was no exception. I reckoned it had to be worth well over £20,000, which would easily clear the debt and give me a bit of change.

That was the upside of the plan.

The downside was that I wasn't convinced that she'd think this was such a great idea, nor did I fancy explaining to her that I was only doing it prevent myself from getting filleted. Obviously, I was thinking about as clearly as the average person thinks when they're as high as a kite on crystal meth. Yet, at the same time I was still together enough to realise that telling her probably wasn't even a remotely sensible idea. So instead, I hatched my masterplan alone.

Although at least my timing was perfect, I wasn't subtle. I pretended to go to work that morning, then waited for my wife to take the kids to school. So far, so good. Right? From this point onwards, however, my 'masterplan' could have done with a little more finesse.

Perhaps I could have slipped 'round the back and quietly broken a window, but instead, I smashed in my own front door in broad daylight, oblivious to the fact that our house was on a residential road and I was doing this in the morning when dozens of people could have easily witnessed my staged burglary. Now that I was 'in', I took around 80 percent of my wife's jewellery before realising that in the least I needed to make this 'robbery' look convincing. With this now in mind, I suddenly decided to ransack the rest of the house, emptying the drawers and scattering the contents all around.

Once that was done I got into my Mercedes and drove to a pawn shop, where I traded the lot for 10 grand, taking a loss of somewhere between £10-15,000. Oddly enough, it didn't even occur to me to be nervous about carrying that kind of cash around. I just went back to my car and drove into London where I paid off the seven grand that I owed. Naturally I then spent a grand of the remaining three on crystal meth.

I was delusional; an addict who failed to think of any of the consequences of my actions that morning. All I cared about was paying these people off to save myself from harm, to protect my family, and to keep feeding my habit. With my debt now cleared, and a grand of crystal meth to my name, this left me with £2,000, so I did what any sensible person would do under the circumstances and headed to a casino.

The best part of this particular gambling outing was that I actually made a bit of money and was feeling generally good about life when I got a phone call. My daughter, then 14, had come back from school, seen the front door open, and had burst into tears. I was so desperate and self-centered that it hadn't even occurred to me that a robbery, even one that I'd faked, would affect her feelings. She called my wife and alerted a neighbour, who in turn called the police. It hadn't occurred to me that this would happen either, which is how delusional I was back then.

While my wife was there, in a state of absolute devastation, the police went 'round the house doing their thing. For her it wasn't even about the money as the jewellery and gold that had been given to her by her mum, her aunties, my mum, and as multiple wedding gifts from varied group of other guests. With nearly all of it now gone, the sentimental damage was incalculable, but they were also frightened to stay in the house in case the robber returned. Yet despite all of their emotional upset, I was as calm as a duck.

Through the use of crystal meth, this was the mindset that I'd achieved. I'd become so skilled at lying that I was even able to convince myself that what I'd just done wasn't actually a robbery at all. I was unable to see that my means of saving my family was actually destroying it. As soon as I got my crystal meth, I was okay; In my head I was able to justify what I'd done and their feelings no longer concerned me.

A few months later the police investigation reached its inevitable conclusion. When I'd pawned the jewellery I'd had to show photographic ID, including my passport, and even the most dull-witted detective could have joined the dots. The police told my wife that I was the culprit and arrested me for robbery. However, it was only when they threatened to arrest *her* for fraudulently claiming on our insurance that I finally came clean.

As I was bang to rights anyway, I didn't have much choice, and while my wife may have been devastated she didn't actually want me to go to jail, so she vouched for me. I was released from Maidstone police station and the charges were dropped.

Whilst in the eyes of the law I was innocent, in the eyes of my family I'd done something they found difficult to forgive. I can't overstate the effect that my actions in this instance had on them... they were absolutely devastated that I could put them through an experience like that.

It was the saddest time in our lives, but it still didn't stop me from behaving like a madman. Somehow I still had a job with Lashings, but I soon remedied that, drinking heavily in the marquees before matches and embarrassing the stars I was supposed to be looking after.

Even thought they didn't know that I was on drugs, because of the way I was acting, David Folb knew that I was no longer right for the job, and with this realisation he let me go.

Now I was left with the few thousand that I'd won from the casino, a family who were disgusted with me, and once again, no job. However, none of this bothered me because as long as I had access to crystal meth, nothing ever would, or could.

12

FLAT LINING

I had maybe a couple of grand left, but with no job and no other source of income, that wasn't going to last long. Belatedly I decided that it was time to do something that would keep my family sweet and tried to go straight by getting more reliable employment.

I wasn't without prospects. I was smartly-dressed, persuasive, charming, eloquent, and reasonably good looking; all of which were ideal qualities in an interview situation. I also has the discipline to stay clean for 24 hours beforehand…getting jobs was easy. It was keeping them that was the difficult bit for me.

Over the next two years I went in and out of various roles. In hindsight the hospitality industry was probably a poor choice of career paths for me to pursue. It's overwhelmingly based in central London and involves "looking after" clients, eating with them, drinking with them, and when the needs of the job demand it, getting off your face with them. It was a role that I also set about with real gusto.

Unable to do anything with restraint, I entered the hospitality industry like Fredo Corleone in *Godfather II*. (Years earlier Marianna Hill, the actress who'd played Fredo's wife Deanna, was my acting coach at the Lee Strasberg Academy.) This was a character that I had more than a little empathy with. Fredo was a talented man who knew how to show someone a good time… and so did I. The problem was that showing someone a Fredo Corleone-style good time in central London was incompatible with a family lifestyle, especially when the last train home was at ten to midnight.

However, unlike me, even Fredo knew that the basic rule of hospitality is to not to enjoy yourself more than your client. I had what seemed like a dream job with a company based in Thanet. The brief was to attend major sporting events and look after clients who had paid for VIP packages. These usually cost somewhere around £4-5000 per head and companies were spending anything up to 50 grand to reward their high-end clients. The trouble for me was that as I'd sold these packages, I thought I had the right to enjoy them as much, if not more, than the clients.

Addicts are great at finding each other and at events like these there's usually a kindred spirit.

I was at Wimbledon when someone offered me some MDMA, more popularly known as ecstasy. Why did I take it? Because, to quote the explorer George Mallory, "it was there." Offer an addict a drug and they'll take it. I remember being impressed by the way it stung my nose when I snorted it. It turned me on and it was something different, but it wasn't as easy to mask the side effects. MDMA makes you sweat… profusely. While I looked like I'd just stepped out of a monsoon shower, at least I could blame it on the heat.

By now I was in my 40s and the immune system that I'd been testing since the age of 11 could no longer cope with the constant load that I'd been placing on it. A few days after Wimbledon, I collapsed while at a family function at which my aunt and uncle were celebrating their anniversary at a five-star hotel near St James Park. While the event was completely dry, I'd started sweating again, so I just sat in a corner, incapable of any kind of socialising and looking like I'd just walked, fully-clothed, out of the shower.

The next thing I remember was waking up in St Mary's Hospital in Paddington, where I was told that I'd flatlined for five seconds in the ambulance before the paramedics finally revived me. While it sounded serious, for whatever reason they released me that night. To this day my family have no idea how close I came to dying, which might be because I carried on as if nothing had happened. Within a day of being discharged I was back on it, downing a couple of bottles of rum. The following summer I was back in the Fredo Corleone role once again, this time at The Open.

The 2015 tournament took place at St Andrews and I was due to fly up the day before from London City airport to Edinburgh — I was drunk before I even got on the plane. On arrival I was met by a driver, a bald eastern European guy whom I immediately hit it off with, partly because he instantly hooked me up with a local drug dealer. I'd barely put my bags down before I was high again. The following morning when I had to go to work I was a wreck.

It's difficult to convince the outside observer that drinking champagne while watching golf even begins to qualify as employment. On a normal day the action does a lot of the work for you, but this was a Scottish summer; it rained incessantly.

Needless to say, the rain had washed out the entire day's play, but I still had clients to entertain. A 50 grand hospitality package includes a lot of "free" champagne and with no chance to relax while everyone else was watching the gold, I consumed it intravenously, in quantities that would have left most of the guests in ruins… but for me it barely touched the sides.

It felt like I was on a ship during a violent storm and I started careening around the marquee, staggering from table-to-table. My brief was to show the clients such a good time that they'd end up booking again for the following year, but all I wanted to do was go to sleep.

Everyone must have known that I was on something, but for one reason or another no one complained. By the time autumn had rolled around, when England was hosting the 2015 Rugby World Cup, I was somehow still employed.

The semi-final between New Zealand and South Africa at Twickenham was a collision between two of the greatest teams ever to have played the game. While it should have been an honour to witness it, once again I was preoccupied hoovering cocaine — and on this specific occasion I'd decided to mix it with crystal meth and dark rum.

Former New Zealand rugby player Zinzan Brooke was the guest speaker in our suite. There's a picture of me a standing next him and it's clear that I'm off my face, although he'd obviously seen it all before and being the pro that he was, he was too polite to say anything.

I'd never left any game early before, but I was in such a state that I slipped away, thinking that I'd catch a train to a family function I was due to attend. However, when I got outside I saw that Twickenham station was closed, so I started walking, in heavy rain, without an umbrella.

Around two hours later I found myself in Putney, drenched and shivering, but just about together enough to realise that I needed to catch a train to another family function where I sat in the corner, yet again, ignoring everyone. Such behaviour heaped even further embarrassment on my wife, who was, by now, being pushed to her breaking point.

Everyone has their limit and I was about discover hers. There is no defence for what I did next. The following week I went out once again, got out of my face once again, and arrived home in the early hours of the following morning. This time things were different as now she refused to let me in. My reaction to this was to start hammering at the door, trying to force it open. When it finally gave way she stood in front of me, refusing to let me past. We were shouting and screaming at each other, and having had enough I finally pushed her out of the way. The force I used sent her flying and she landed on her back, damaging it quite seriously. While this could have paralysed her, I still managed to see myself as the victim.

Due to all of the noise of our argument, the neighbours had been awakened and summarily called the police. Having made a series of indefensible decisions in the course of the evening, I now made another one and decided to drive off. However, by this point I was so impaired that I immediately slammed it into reverse and smashed into a neighbour's car.

When it came to evading capture I was anything but the Scarlet Pimpernel. I'd barely made it 'round the corner when I parked up and decided that it was time to kill myself by taking all my pills. I had around 5000mg of bipolar meds, quetiapine and lamotrigine, and I took the whole lot in one go.

While these were both heavy drugs in their own right, I probably didn't really want to die because almost immediately I realised what I'd done and started jamming my fingers down my throat.

The next thing I remember was being in another ambulance, but this time with a police escort. I went to A&E, where I was detoxed, but as soon as I was out of danger I was arrested, charged with domestic violence, and taken to a jail cell.

Obviously this was an incredibly traumatic time; in hindsight I can also understand how all of this must have seemed to the neighbours. However, I can honestly say that while I may have been guilty of many things — and I have no doubt that I put my wife, Mehz through hell — I'd never intended to physically hurt her. As much as she had every right to hate me at that point, she also knew that what had happened was an accident.

After 36 hours I was released and the charges were dropped. Whether or not I deserved it, I'd still been given another chance.

Once again, I blew it.

———

In my lucid moments I could still act like a successful human being, but after outstaying my welcome in the hospitality industry I needed another job. By now I knew the drill. I could stay clean for 24 hours before the interview, turn up in my best suit, looking like a Wall Street player and charm my way into nearly any position that I fancied.

I now applied for a role with a global asset management company based on Liverpool Street. The first interview went brilliantly and I was invited back for a second one a couple of days later. Yet this time I encountered a senior executive who clearly didn't like the look of me. In fact, he was at the point of bombing me out when I found out that he was a Spurs supporter — picking this up, I casually mentioned that we shared the same faith.

While I can't be 100 percent certain that this tipped the balance in my favor, his mood towards me definitely shifted with this mention and to my surprise I was in.

To an outside observer it would have looked like a dream job. I got to travel all over Europe looking after clients and selling estate pensions. For a while I managed to hold things together, but choosing to abstain was merely a short-term solution that punted the problem down the road for a while. If you don't admit you're an addict, the option to resume drinking is always there... and sooner or later you'll cave in. This is the logic — if you don't have a problem, why shouldn't you have a drink?

In that kind of working environment, temptation was never more than one, lonely evening in a hotel away.

If you're in an airport and you have two hours to kill before a flight there's always a bar; it's one of the few places where drinking before noon seems to be universally accepted. Yet through all of this I managed to steer clear of drink and drugs until we had a company boat party on the Thames, just by Tower Bridge. And at this party I just got mashed off my face.

The vessel looked a bit like a pirate ship and as the alcohol was once again free, I drank like a sailor, hammering the complimentary booze, then disappearing to a miniscule toilet whenever I needed a substance that was beyond the limits of legality.

Once again I didn't go home that night. Instead, I woke up on the floor of a hotel to find that both the police and an ambulance crew had forced their way into the room. What I didn't understand was why they were ignoring *me*. It was only when I noticed that the chap on the floor next to me was overdosing on heroin that I realised they weren't there for me. Even though it was the middle of the night, I sheepishly rang my wife and she came to pick me up.

Still unable to grasp the indisputable fact that I was an addict, and still ignoring all of the warning klaxons and flashing red lights, *I carried on as if nothing had happened.* I still went to parties, still binged on anything I could get my hands on, still ignored food, and worst of all, still refused to take my bipolar medication. As a result, I lost too much weight and further drove away those who were closest to me.

I transferred money from my wife's account to my own, blowing it on drink, drugs, and gambling. At work I took ludicrous risks. One of my responsibilities was staff training and I'd host video-conference calls, during which I would duck my head down and snort a line that I'd racked out on the table. While the people I was talking to might not have been able to see the cocaine in front of me, they were certainly able to see my eyes popping out of my skull when my head bobbed back up again.

Although I got away with that, the situation was unsustainable. I was approaching my life in the same way that a number 11 batsman approaches an inning in a test match... flailing away at delivery after delivery, skying a few to the boundary, nicking a few past the fielders, and somehow staying in. The only certainty was that, sooner rather than later, I was going to get caught.

The following week, already high on coke and crystal meth from a binge the day before, I accompanied my boss to Berlin. The evening started pleasantly enough as we checked into the Sofitel on Kurfürstendamm, had drinks on a rooftop terrace, and had dinner in an Italian restaurant.

Some time after this we had a falling out. While I can't remember exactly why, I think it was something to do with his refusal to give me cash. For some reason I found his unwillingness to fund my drug habit objectionable and we had a bit of an argument.

Already very heavily drunk, I found it easy to make new best friends... and my new best friends knew where I could find everything I needed to get even further off my face than I was already.

Unfortunately I also found it easy to make new enemies as well. I got into an altercation that saw me end up in a police cell, where instead of feeling shame, all I could think of was how impressively clean it was in there. I can honestly say that it was the nicest cell I've ever been in, which probably says something about my overall mindset at the time.

Yet, the *Polizei* didn't give me long to enjoy my new surroundings; when they finally released me it almost felt like a let down. A part of me had wanted to get caught. It was the same when I used to drive while under the influence. There was always a risk of getting caught, but I accepted it, reasoning that if I did get banned at least I wouldn't have to drive any more.

Getting caught gave me an excuse. It also took matters out my hands.

This mindset explains what happened next. That night my boss had seen me at my very worst — he knew that I'd been arrested and didn't say a word to me during the entire journey home.

The silence was only broken when we reached Gatwick. He thought it was a normal working day and, somewhat incredibly, given what had happened the night before, was expecting me to go back to the office with him. Whether or not he was planning to sack me when I got there, to this day I don't know. However, when I told him that I was going home to sleep, it was only then that I was fired — an outcome that I'm fairly sure I'd been trying to engineer all along.

I went home and slept for three days. When I emerged I learned that my daughter had booked me an appointment at a drug and alcohol rehabilitation centre in Maidstone.

My life, as I knew it, was over.

13

ADDICTED TO RECOVERY

Berlin was the last time that I've ever touched either drink or drugs. While I'm immensely proud, and equally grateful, that my eldest child was smart enough to make this life-saving intervention, it's also important for me to be one hundred percent truthful about how I felt at the time.

My initial reaction was cynical. I knew that my family were acting out of love, and for that reason I also knew that I had to keep them happy. I thought I could play along for a while, and after a suitable period of penance, I could more than likely resume my previous lifestyle. While I made all the right noises, all the while I assumed that this was just going to be a set of tick-box exercises.

However, as soon as I attended my first session this plan went out of the window.

My rebirth took place in a three-storey office building in Mill Street, Maidstone, surrounded by fellow addicts from every walk of life.

There were builders, bankers, long-term unemployed individuals, ex-gangsters, and even a DJ. However, in spite of their diverse backgrounds, this being Maidstone, with the exception of me they were all exclusively white.

The meetings were hosted by recovering addicts who understood exactly what we were going through. They also knew *all* of the bullshit excuses that addicts can and will come up with to justify their behaviour. I represented a classic case of denial.

My mentor saw right through me. I was a brilliant liar and although I never made it as an actor I'd always been able to put on a convincing show when I'd needed to mask my addictions. She knew my condition better than I did; as soon as I spoke to her something inside me broke.

Suddenly I experienced a complete emotional capitulation and broke down, sobbing uncontrollably for a solid twenty minutes. When I'd finally regained my composure I took stock of my new surroundings.

There were various fellowships — the most common is Alcoholics Anonymous — but there were also others for cocaine, gambling, crystal meth, and even sex.

This was my introduction to the 12 step programme.

While this is extensively covered elsewhere, it's worth repeating the core principles, in this instance, of Alcoholics Anonymous.

1. We admitted we were powerless over alcohol — that our lives had become unmanageable.
2. We came to believe that a Power greater than ourselves could restore us to sanity.
3. We made a decision to turn our will and our lives over to the care of God as we understood Him.

4. We made a searching and fearless moral inventory of ourselves.

5. We admitted to God, to ourselves and to another human being the exact nature of our wrongs.

6. We were entirely ready to have God remove all these defects of character.

7. We humbly asked Him to remove our shortcomings.

8. We made a list of all persons we had harmed, and became willing to make amends to them all.

9. We made direct amends to such people wherever possible, except when to do so would injure them or others.

10. We continued to take personal inventory and when we were wrong promptly admitted it.

11. We sought through prayer and meditation to improve our conscious contact with God as we understood Him, praying only for knowledge of His will for us and the power to carry that out.

12. Having had a spiritual awakening as the result of these steps, we tried to carry this message to alcoholics and to practice these principles in all our affairs.

I was told this was a spiritual programme and not a religious one, so for a lapsed Muslim like myself, step 11 with the words, "God as we understood him," was perhaps the key to making sense of it.

Step 12 was my way out.

Recovery was something that I found myself embracing very quickly, to the point of it becoming my new addiction.

I went to meetings daily — sometimes twice a day — and was also having a community detox at the same time. The results were rapid. There's a detox facility in Maidstone called Bridge House and I'd been promised a bed there, but by the time one became available I turned it down. The 12 step-programme and the detox were proving to be so effective that I already felt that somebody else needed that bed more than I did.

After a year of attending meetings, reading voraciously, and making amends with the people I'd wronged, I now felt that I was able to pass on what I'd learned and use my experiences to help others.

I went for an interview with the RAPt organisation, now known as Forward Trust, and landed a role as an apprentice drug and alcohol practitioner at HMP Swaleside, a Category B prison on the Isle of Sheppey — a brief, amazing, and yet bizarre experience.

HMP Swaleside is the kind of jail where 'life' means *life*. It was there where I found myself surrounded by some very serious offenders. Once again, they came from a variety of different backgrounds, but by now I'd learned that *addiction does not discriminate*. There were those who had vast bank balances and others who were destitute. Some looked like catwalk models, others tramps; some had high-flying careers, others were unemployable.

Yet, while they came from every ethnic background, every religion, and spoke multiple languages, we all had one common goal: the willingness to get clean. The room was full of people like me, people I could relate to who could also relate to me.

There was also a gangster element present, the type that I'd always got a thrill from mingling with. There were IRA sympathisers, murderers, drug traffickers, and Somali gang members; many of whom were just young kids who'd been forced into doing things that they'd never wanted to do.

At the end of every meeting we recited something called the Serenity Prayer, in which we ask:

"God grant us the serenity to accept the things we cannot change, the courage to change the things that we can, and the wisdom to know the difference. Amen."

We held hands while saying it aloud together. I remember that on my first day there I felt like we were in some kind of cult. While at first it was quite difficult for me to comprehend, there was a sense of communion present in this group... a sense of collectiveness and togetherness, all of which I liked.

I remember there was a murderer, who was really hostile at first. He said "I don't shut my eyes, I don't do this bollocks." However, by the end, even he was won over.

I was totally at ease with all of them, with one exception. My personal history made me distinctly uncomfortable for me to sit in a room with the paedophiles and rapists in the sex offenders wing. For their own safety they were kept apart from the rest of the other inmates... their mindset made it very difficult to get through to them.

Triage is an essential part of the rehabilitation process and everyone is asked if they feel that they've hurt anyone. When you ask a murderer or a drug trafficker this question, nine times out ten they'll say 'yes'. However, sex offenders invariably say 'no'. As someone who'd been abused earlier in my life, I found this attitude to be most bizarre. In spite of my inner feelings, I carried on working with them because I knew that they were going to be released, sooner rather than later, and I felt that I could play a part in convincing them not to reoffend.

On one occasion I dealt with a Punjabi guy who didn't seem to be taking in a word that I'd said, however, at the end of the session he shook my hand. I remember feeling so disgusted by this simple act that once I made it back to the relative sanctuary of the drug wing, I scrubbed my hands incessantly like Lady Macbeth. I felt dirty and filthy; it was a profound experience. It wasn't so much talking with the sex offender, preparing the treatment plan, or listening to their stories, but the actual handshake at the end that really got to me. I'll never forget that day. I don't know whether it was because I was abused, or because he was so open about what he'd done, but there were times when I found it impossible to remain non-judgmental.

I was never tempted to quit because, that aside, I loved my work. Yet after a few months I was summoned to the governor's room. He told me that he'd seen one of my talks, in which I talked about my journey and my message of hope. Then he "asked me to leave" on the grounds that I represented a risk to the offenders.

I was absolutely gobsmacked and shattered… especially when I found out that the talk that so upset them had been recorded by a colleague of mine… one who obviously didn't like me very much either. As an added 'bonus', I was caught on camera being hugged by a prisoner… something that was strictly forbidden. In terms of boundaries, I actually agree that you shouldn't have physical contact with inmates. However, it was done so quickly, and in such a sincere manner on his part, that I couldn't really have stopped him. I suppose I could have tried to argue that it was an assault, but it wouldn't have made a lot of difference. In all honesty, he'd only been trying to show his appreciation for the work that I'd been doing with them. No matter what, they wanted me out… and the rejection was *devastating*.

In fact, this was a dangerous time when I was especially vulnerable to relapsing. When I'd had similar setbacks in the past, such as when I'd left Lashings, I'd tried to submerge my sorrows in substance abuse, but this time I didn't. It was a measure of the progress that I'd made that I was more into my recovery than any drug.

A brief spell at HMP Rochester followed, where I once again felt I was making a difference; but was once again asked to leave when the authorities were alerted to my message of hope. I think the charity was nearly as surprised as I was, yet I sometimes wonder if the staff resented the fact that I'd never served jail time for the things that

I openly admitted that I'd done. However, this is not something that I choose to dwell on anymore.

Once again, it was time to reinvent myself. However this time, having finally learned from the mistakes of my past, I chose an upward path.

14

FILLING IN THE BLANKS

By now I'm sure that most of you reading my story have a few questions to ask me. It's because of this that I thought that I'd take the time to address some of the more obvious ones for you in an effort to help you to both better understand addiction as well as filling in some of the blanks that were left in the rest of the book.

First of all, I'm sure that there are a few of you who wonder if being adopted had anything to do with the drive I felt to use illicit substances. This is also a question that I had since I began to put all of the pieces of my addiction puzzle together.

Studies in the United States — which I've read, but am not able to cite for you at this moment — have found that adopted children are at a greater risk of experiencing emotional and behavioural problems than children who remained with their birth parents. Previous research has also found that children who were older at the time of their adoption were more likely to experience both emotional and behavioural problems.

A controversial term, Adopted Child Syndrome, has been used to explain certain kinds of behaviour that's expressed by those who've been adopted. Specifically, these include:

- Problems with bonding   (check)
- Attachment disorders   (check)
- Lying   (check)
- Defiance of Authority   (check)
- Acts of Violence   (check)

In addition, they also include:

- Problems with developing an identity
- Reduced self-esteem and self-confidence
- An increased risk of substance abuse
- Higher rates of mental health disorders (such as depression and PTSD)

Of the above, I'm "guilty" on all counts.

In the end, the findings of the study have postulated that adoption itself is a form of trauma. Without the biological connection to their mother, even newborns can feel that something is wrong. As a result of this subtly sensed lacking they can be difficult to soothe. This effect has the potential to grow over time… even in the most loving and supportive of adoptive homes, like mine.

Over time, my relationship with my adoptive mum became one that was very close. Once she told me about my adoption our relationship didn't change outwardly, but I was still affected by this revelation and resented her for not telling me sooner.

I didn't care to look for either of my birth parents and it was only after my adopted mum and dad had passed that I started to look for them. Fortunately by the time I began this process I had entered recovery. As of this writing, I'm awaiting the birth certificate that my adoptive parents told me I never had. Even though that was not true,

I now believe that I can understand why they felt they had to deceive me.

In the short term after being given the news of my adoption, I coped in the only way that I knew how... by leaving the house that night and buying a bottle of vodka, which I drank without any hesitation.

A few places in the book I made mention of either ceasing, or refusing, to take my bipolar medication... something that took place much later in my story.

At the age of 42 (approximately eight years ago as of this writing in 2021), I was finally diagnosed with bipolar disorder. It happened in a somewhat 'accidental' manner (even though I believe that there are no accidents). My wife and daughter were watching an Indian talk show, *Satyamev Jayate*, that was hosted by the Bollywood actor, Aamir Khan. The particular episode that they both happened to be watching together dealt with mental health and bipolarity and as a result of this, they asked me to visit a community mental health team where I was tested and duly diagnosed. Finally I was beginning to get more pieces that seemed to fit my own puzzle... I just had to fit them in.

However, this was somewhere between 2012 and 2013, or three to four years before my arrest in Berlin which finally led to my sobriety. Needless to say, at the time of this discovery I was still in the throes of my addictions. The problem with this diagnosis was that it led to more medication... quetiapine, to be specific.

Quetiapine is an antipsychotic medication that's used to treat schizophrenia, bipolar disorder, and major depressive order in adults, along with a host of other conditions. The problem for me was that taking this med turned me into a *zombie*. As you may be able to imagine, it didn't help that I was still dosing myself on a regular basis with crystal meth, cocaine, and alcohol. Worse yet, when I stopped taking the medication, I did so abruptly without reducing the dosage slowly over ten days or so. As a result, the side effects of this were so strong that I became 'scatty.'

Still unable to grasp that I was an addict, and continuing to ignore all of the warning klaxons and flashing red lights, I carried on as if nothing had happened... going to parties, binging on anything I could get my hands on, ignoring food and losing weight, and driving away those closest to me in the process.

Once sober, I finally paid attention to this condition and got the proper medication, which was yet another step in the proper direction for my life to heal.

My studies in Addiction Psychology, along with my work with both Dr. Demartini and TJ Woodward, were a great help to my healing, as was my work with my sponsor in 12 Step recovery. However, in the process of my recovery, I learned so much about addiction that I feel both empowered and driven to help others who are still trapped in addiction as I once was. It is to this end that I dedicate my work outside of my home and personal life. Inside my home, I dedicate myself to loving my family in the healthiest way possible.

One thing is for sure... I am grateful and blessed.

EPILOGUE

SURVIVE, OVERCOME, AND THRIVE

While I'm proud to say that I'm a survivor, I now believe that I am so much more.

It's no small miracle that I've survived – both the racial abuse that I and my parents were subjected to from as early as I can remember, and the sexual abuse that was endemic at the boarding school I attended for six years. After years of struggle, I finally also overcame the resulting addictions that nearly killed me – both physically and spiritually.

August 11th, 2016 was the first day of the rest of my life and I have been thriving ever since. I haven't touched alcohol or narcotics since my arrest in Berlin and I can honestly say that I no longer have any desire to do so.

While my experiences with the prison service were initially a setback, they ultimately made me stronger. From there I did volunteer work with the children's society and worked with Christingle, one of the oldest charities in the UK, to help addicts on the streets. I worked in a homeless shelter during Christmastime, and felt happier with this new, altruistic lifestyle than I ever had when I was high.

I continued to read everything and anything that I could get my hands on. As a result of an inner desire to help others in a more formalized manner, I started to study for my masters degree in Addiction Psychology. Along the way I've also studied the *Breakthrough Experience* with Dr. John Demartini, as well as receiving training from in Conscious Recovery created by TJ Woodward.

Fueled by my desire to continue communicating my message of hope to a broader audience, I started a weekly radio show called *Saf's Surgery,* a programme dedicated to helping alleviate and heal addiction trauma and mental health that's broadcast every Sunday night on the new Maidstone Community Radio station.

In turn, this led to a job with Sky TV where I became the host of a men's talk show on Feelgood Factor TV, one that's been a phenomenal success overall. From this platform, I now get to communicate my message of hope to a far wider audience than I ever could have had I simply continued to lecture in prisons... even though on its own, that was a very rewarding experience.

In spite of all of this newfound success, my greatest achievement has been the opportunity to become a husband and a father again... one that I wholeheartedly embrace. After everything that I put my family through, they were willing to forgive me – and for this I can say that my gratitude is unending.

I spent much of my life before recovery captivated by gangsters and the way that they lived. As a result, this book is peppered with references to those films that I loved... films that romanticised such a lifestyle.

The greatest gangster movie of all time, perhaps the greatest film of all time, is *The Godfather.* However, it couldn't have achieved such a level of greatness if the violence hadn't been accompanied by a love story – that of one man for his family.

When Johnny Fontaine begs Vito Corleone for a "favour" on his daughter's wedding day, he grants his wish, but as he does he also offers him some advice.

"A man who doesn't spend time with his family can never be a real man."

This is a lesson that I learned later than most, whilst earlier than some. Yet I'm forever grateful that I learned it before it was too late.

CONNECTING WITH ME

As I began to discover my options for helping others by communicating my message of hope, I started the weekly radio programme, Saf's Surgery, on the new Maidstone Community Radio station. As it had started off on a small scale, in a radio station that was run and funded entirely by volunteers, I didn't anticipate that this would lead to any kind of broadcasting career. However, since the show was brutally honest and resonated with so many people, our audience began to snowball into something I'd never imagined.

From there what we were doing began to be noticed by more and more and subsequently I was asked to audition for a Sky TV show on Feel Good Factor TV. As the name implies, the station is supposed to be an antidote to the diet of misery that's broadcast by the mainstream media. I saw this as an opportunity to communicate my message to a far wider audience than I ever could have if I would have simply continued to lecture in prisons.

My show, "Men's Talk," is a discussion programme in which we talk about a variety of issues, but always with the same guiding philosophy:

- You don't have to give in to addiction.
- Your present does not have to be overshadowed by your past.
- There is a better future for you if you have the discipline to pursue it.

In addition to the show, I speak to groups in a similar manner as I do on the show. I also work as a coach on an individual basis, in which I run a series of Behavioural Coaching sessions that are tailored to each individual client.

I'm also part of the online community known as Spiritually Gone Wild, where individuals can find a wide variety of personal and spiritual growth tools, countless hours of content, and a collection of free and paid courses that you can use to raise your vibration and lift your soul energy as high as you dare go.

To contact me, book me for either a speaking engagement or a guest spot on your show or podcast, or to work with me one-on-one, all of this can be accomplished through my website:

www.safbuxy.com

ABOUT THE AUTHOR

Saf Buxy is a Social Behavioural Mentor and Addiction Specialist. He is an Author, Speaker, TV, Radio and Social Media personality, and respected pioneer in Addiction Consulting. He delivers life-changing material and personal expertise to shift clients towards a more fulfilling future.

Through gaining personal empirical knowledge, Saf Buxy incorporates this experience along with research, training, and vocation in guiding those afflicted by trauma and addiction. The complexity of human behaviour requires a non-prescriptive approach; Saf transforms people's lives through mentally disbanding the cause of their pain.

As a proponent of breaking free from 'the madness', Saf has successfully liberated numberless individuals from tribulation so that they continue to lead a fruitful and inspiring life.

Saf would love to connect and hear from readers! He can be reached at info@safbuxy.com.

For further resources created especially for his readers, visit:
www.SafBuxy.com/madnessgift

www.Saf Buxy.com

Printed in Great Britain
by Amazon